THE BLACKS IN OKLAHOMA
by Jimmie Lewis Franklin

Oklahoma Image is a project sponsored by the
Oklahoma Department of Libraries
and the Oklahoma Library Association,
and made possible by a grant from the
National Endowment for the Humanities.

Library of Congress Cataloging in Publication Data

Franklin, Jimmie Lewis.
  The Blacks in Oklahoma

  (Newcomers to a new land)
  Bibliography: p.
  1. Afro-Americans — Oklahoma — History.   2. Oklahoma —
History.   I. Title.   II. Series.
  E185.93.O4F72   976.6'004'96073   79-24318

ISBN 978-0-8061-1671-6 (paper)

CONTENTS

To Reverend William Harkless, Reneé, and Marvin

PREFACE

Permanent black settlement in Oklahoma dates from the 1830s, although a few blacks came with early explorers many years prior to the formation of the Sooner State. When the federal government removed the so-called Five Civilized Tribes (Choctaws, Cherokees, Creeks, Seminoles, Chickasaws) from their homes in the southeastern portion of the United States to free lands for the advancing cotton frontier, the Indians brought their black slaves with them to their new homes in the West. As in the Deep South these blacks tilled the soil, carried out domestic chores, planted and harvested crops, and performed other duties for their Indian masters. Emancipation, of course, came during the American Civil War, and following that terrible conflict the new freedmen of Indian Territory became members of the various tribes. They also received allotments of lands. When President Benjamin Harrison opened a section of what is now Oklahoma to settlement in 1889, other blacks, principally from the South and from Kansas, came to the region. At the formation of Oklahoma Territory blacks represented over 8 percent of the population and their numbers continued to grow until the years of the Great Depression. While the thirties witnessed a decline in the number of black citizens in the state, the total population gradually climbed back toward the level it had occupied in previous years. Today, of a total population of 2.5 million people, blacks constitute close to 180,000, nearly half of whom live in the metropolitan areas of Oklahoma City and Tulsa.

This work is tailored for the general reader, and combines narrative with enough interpretation to make it palatable to persons from different backgrounds, and to serious students of history who desire a brief account of the subject. The book focuses upon central themes that have pervaded the history of black Oklahomans, and upon influential personalities who have been responsible for fostering a sense of community, racial solidarity, and progress among blacks in the state. As much as the sources permit, the author emphasizes an institutional approach to the survey of black life. Through the examination of institutions the historian can best comprehend the pathos of black existence. Through them he can watch the unfolding quest for a sense of community, racial equality, and identity. The study here examines the history of blacks from within a relatively circumscribed community to determine what it says about itself and, perhaps just as important, what it suggests about the structure of the larger society outside.

Focus assumes significance in a work of this nature. For most of the state's history Jim Crowism occupied a central place in the life of Oklahoma's black community. This book, however, is much broader than segregation. The trials and challenges of everyday existence as well as the joys and pleasures of daily life constitute important portions of the moving drama of blacks in the Sooner state. This is not racial history that concentrates unduly upon contributions of a particular group in almost total isolation from larger historical developments. Indeed, scores of noted black Oklahomans do move across the pages of this study—some more swiftly than others—but they are usually part of the fascinating story of a black community in search of a solution to the problems which consistently confronted it.

Many generous people aided me in writing this short survey. I regret that I cannot mention all of them. At least a score of librarians at colleges and universities gave freely of their services. The staff at the Oklahoma Historical Society, especially Manon Atkins and Mary Moran, showed much patience in responding to my request for documents and newspapers. I would also like to thank the Oklahoma Image Advisory Committee—The Honorable Hannah Atkins, Ruby Ewing, Rubye Hall, Russell Perry and Jimmy Stewart—for its help. The friendship of four colleagues and friends—Dean James Johnson, Herbert Alexander, Bill T. Ridgeway and J. Elmer Pullen—kept me sane. My chairman, Robert Hennings, did not bother me with the petty details that prey upon one's time and stifle progress. Since his arrival at Eastern Illinois University, President Daniel Marvin has strongly supported my research and writing efforts. I am grateful to him. Finally, I want to thank my wife, Golda, who endured.

Eastern Illinois University   *Jimmie Lewis Franklin*

Chapter 1

LIFE IN A NEW LAND

Many miles separate the southeastern section of the United States from the state of Oklahoma. Even with today's speedy modes of transportation, the distance seems imposing for those who desire to travel from, say, Georgia to Oklahoma. Any suggestion that a person attempt such a journey *on horseback* or *in a wagon* would doubtless bring a smile if not outright laughter. People, of course, are conditioned by their times, their culture, and the things around them. For those who lived in the early nineteenth century a proposed trip by horse or wagon would not have appeared a "crazy" idea. To the Five Civilized Tribes of Indians—Choctaws, Cherokees, Chickasaws, Creeks, Seminoles—who lived in the American Southeast the suggestion of a trip by such means was indeed disturbing, but not necessarily because of the method of transportation. It bothered them most because the government wanted to remove the Indians and their black slaves from their land. It is at this point that the exciting story of Oklahoma's permanent black population must logically begin; and it is necessary to step back briefly into time to properly understand it.

The desire to grow cotton in the early nineteenth century and the advancing westward movement of white Americans created a need for valuable land. With the invention of the gin, cotton became enormously profitable, and by the 1820s white farmers had begun to pressure the government for cheaper acreage. They also wanted to expand into the southeast. More land meant more rewards for farmers who sold cotton to New Englanders or to the British who used it in the manufacture of textiles. Expansion into this region, however, encountered a problem. Upon this land the Five Civilized Tribes had established homes, grown crops, reared families, and created a culture. They had also developed the institution of slavery,

1

much like the whites of the South. For years the Indians and their slaves remained virtually undisturbed, but their lives changed radically when the federal government yielded to farmers' demands for more land. With strong leadership from the federal government, particularly President Andrew Jackson, the United States adopted a removal policy in 1830, although a few Indians had come west before that time. In providing for new homes for the Indians the government set aside what eventually became Indian Territory, comprising most of what is now the state of Oklahoma.

Hardship and much heartache attended the removal of the Indians to the West. The slaves who came with them suffered along with their masters and experienced the terrible ordeal upon the "Trail of Tears," a descriptive phrase used to denote the long, grueling journey the Indians and blacks made to Oklahoma. It would have been difficult enough to move under the most favorable circumstances. Leaving one's home, especially for the unfamiliar, has never been easy for any people. And it was particularly trying for a group being forced from lands and surroundings they knew so well. Removal represented a harsh fate for the Indians who had lived upon their lands in perfect freedom. The conditions under which many of them moved caused added bitterness and pain. Many Choctaws and their slaves, for example, came to their new homes in midwinter when temperatures fell below zero. Some had to march through heavy snow. Cholera and other diseases took their toll of both Indians and slaves, so that perhaps a fourth of them died along the Trail of Tears. The story of the Cherokees was a harsh picture of death and misery, but none of the Five Civilized Tribes and their slaves escaped completely the suffering that came with their being uprooted. Not until the United States had conducted a costly war against the Seminoles, who bitterly opposed any move West, did removal come to an end in the early 1840s. The defeat of that tribe and their journey to Oklahoma culminated a dark period in American history.

Removal took the lives of many along the Trail of Tears, but it did not kill slavery. Just how many blacks came with the tribes cannot be accurately determined, although the number who lived in Indian Territory at the time of the Civil War exceeded 7,000. The institution of slavery proved much milder in Indian Territory than in the American South. Slave tasks greatly resembled the work of a farmhand or that of a domestic servant. Slavery in Indian Territory has sometimes been compared to indentured servitude of an earlier period in American history. The absence of large-scale plantations, such as

Black slave of Choctaw plantation owner, Indian Territory. Courtesy of the Oklahoma Historical Society.

those of the Deep South, aided in lessening the slaves' workload and the harshness of bondage. But cotton production among the tribes was much larger than some writers previously assumed and slaves did a lot of the backbreaking work. Some people dismiss any discussion of the relative harshness of slavery, contending that human bondage itself amounted to brutality. Whatever the arguments about

3

the nature of slavery, abolitionists in Indian Territory opposed the institution. Not surprisingly, they met strong opposition and some tribes passed legislation which excluded them from their lands. Blacks themselves occasionally registered their disapproval of slavery through revolt or running away.

Freedom for black slaves did not come until the aftermath of the American Civil War. During that contest black soldiers had played a significant part in achieving victory for the Union. Some of the black troops of the Tenth Calvary later helped to build the commissary at Fort Sill, Oklahoma. The success of black and white troops and military necessity made certain the emancipation of blacks in Indian Territory and the South. Although President Abraham Lincoln issued the Emancipation Proclamation in 1863, slavery did not effectively end in the territory until three years later. At that time federal officials and representatives of the Five Civilized Tribes met at Fort Smith, Arkansas, to hammer out details of a peace treaty. The government argued that the Indians had sided with the Confederacy and should be punished. Although they had actually been split in their allegiance between North and South, the federal government required the tribes to relinquish a large part of their territory for the possible settlement of other Indians. Among other things, the treaty also specified that the Indians grant former slaves—freedmen—allotments of land, and they were to become members of the tribes. The government's efforts to provide newly freed blacks a means of earning a living by insuring them land was important, for it helped to avoid the dire poverty witnessed among blacks in many parts of the Deep South. Had the central government adopted a similar policy for the rest of the nation during the period following the war, the history of the relationship between the races might have been different. Some Indians, of course, balked at the idea of giving their ex-slaves parcels of land, but eventually most blacks received an allotment of from 40 to 160 acres. Choctaws and Chickasaws preferred the removal of blacks from within their domain, and the latter ultimately refused to accept blacks as full-fledged members of their tribe.

Prior to the Civil War the black population of Indian Territory consisted of slaves and a small number of so-called free Negroes. The opening of Indian and government lands after the struggle between North and South led to the migration of other blacks to the region. The frontier offered the possibility of economic hope and advancement. And blacks with the resources to move were as attracted by a chance out West as were whites determined to find their

Jimmie Lewis Franklin

Black soldiers guarding David L. Payne and "boomers." Courtesy of the Western
History Collections, University of Oklahoma Library.

place in the sun. When the American government opened for settlement a section called the Unassigned Lands, blacks came along with
the hundreds who took part in a dramatic run to stake out a home-
stead. They came from near and far to this land where black troops,
called Buffalo Soldiers, had assisted in keeping out intruders until
President Benjamin Harrison opened it in 1889. For a time, blacks
who gathered to take part in the run experienced equality on Oklahoma's frontier, for the government did not permit any discrimination
against those who wanted to take part in the run. Exactly how many
blacks participated in the historic run is not known, but when the
starting signal sounded they were there—on foot and horseback,
and in wagons. Lizzie Robinson and her parents came from Memphis
with a group of blacks, all of whom later acquired homesteads. Peter
O'Flynn made the run by horseback on 22 April and successfully
staked out a claim near El Reno in Canadian County. More black
pioneers joined the '89ers when the government opened other lands
to settlement. By 1900 Indian Territory and Oklahoma Territory,
the latter established in 1890, contained more than 55,000 blacks.

5

Black settlers had to demonstrate industry and intelligence to survive on a tough frontier. Hopeful and enthusiastic blacks, many of them from the American South, sometimes arrived without much money or the tools to adapt to a new life, a life strikingly different from that of their native home. Most made the adjustment and became productive citizens who established homes and families. Some, tragically, returned home. W. G. Taylor was one settler who came to Oklahoma and stayed. He arrived in 1892, acquired 160 acres of good land, and began farming and raising chickens. Suffering from loneliness on his isolated farm, Taylor temporarily left his home, went to Missouri, found a wife, and then brought her back to Oklahoma Territory. Much like Taylor, many early black settlers lived in dugouts. Roscoe Dungee, the famous editor of the Oklahoma City *Black Dispatch,* saw many dugouts when his family arrived in Oklahoma Territory in the 1890s. For a young boy from Minnesota, where people used timber and brick, a dugout struck him as strange. Fortunately, the young Dungee had a minister for a father who built a frame house, the very type which became common with the passage of the Oklahoma frontier.

The work of black boosters who promoted the future state of Oklahoma as a land of promise greatly accounted for an increase in population. Among the most celebrated of all boosters was Edward McCabe. Born in 1850 to poor parents in Troy, New York, McCabe received most of his education in New England. When his father died the young man left school to support his family. He went to Chicago, but the West beckoned. He eventually went to Kansas in the 1870s where he soon became heavily involved in the politics of the Republican party. In his early thirties, McCabe ran for the office of state auditor. He won—and in a Kansas that had very few blacks! When his party failed to renominate him, McCabe departed Kansas for California. In 1889 opportunity again appeared, but this time on the horizon to the East—in Oklahoma. McCabe arrived in Guthrie, purchased 160 acres of land about eleven miles east of that city, and then proceeded to establish a town he called Langston in honor of the black United States congressman from Virginia who served after the Civil War. He also started a paper, the Langston *Herald* to promote his town, and dispatched agents to the South to woo black settlers. McCabe wanted to insure that Langston remained all black. He reputedly tried to see that land titles could never pass to a white person, or that no white could ever reside or conduct business in the town.

Jimmie Lewis Franklin

Black pioneer family on claim with dugout, near Guthrie. Courtesy of the Western History Collections, University of Oklahoma Library.

McCabe had more in mind than the establishment of Langston. He wanted to make Oklahoma into a black state, but from the beginning the scheme encountered difficulty. Most whites disliked the idea, and some blacks thought it unworkable. Those who doubted McCabe's plan said he could not possibly devise a way for blacks to be a majority or attain a political balance of power in Oklahoma Territory. When he expressed a desire to become governor of Oklahoma Territory, black state or not, the serious concern whites had shown became alarm. Many of them warned that they had no intention of living under the leadership of a black person, and that they could not accept "domination" by a "Negro government." Black rule, in their judgment, would invariably attract black people from the South, and that would not serve their interest. Some stated frankly that a McCabe governorship would lead to bloodshed. Violence, however, did not come because McCabe's bid failed. Actually, his black-state scheme and his desire for the governorship never had much chance of success. A much larger white population in Oklahoma Territory, an inability to attract massive numbers of blacks, and the existence of racism, all helped to shatter McCabe's dreams. McCabe received only weak support from the Republican party for his governorship bid, although he remained firmly attached to it. The party later appointed him to serve as deputy territorial auditor, the first black to occupy a major political office in the West. McCabe left Oklahoma when the Democrats swept the Republicans from office at the beginning of statehood.

McCabe's boosterism and that of later promoters not only encouraged new settlement but also contributed to the growth of some of the all-black towns in the territories. Several of these communities dated from the pre-Civil War era, but the creation of the two most noted of Oklahoma's twenty-seven known black towns, Langston and Boley, came much later. Langston, McCabe's handiwork, never became a large city, possessing only a population of a few hundred by statehood. But it had become the home of Langston University in 1897. Boley also had an exciting beginning. Founded in 1903 and named for W. H. Boley, a worker for a railroad company, the city rapidly became a thriving community and a center for social activities. By 1907 churches, schools, fraternal lodges, and other institutions provided evidence of a vibrant culture. Businesses, including a bank, developed to satisfy the needs of the community. Those who visited Boley in the early years of her existence praised the town's progress, and applauded the diligence and the industry of her citizens.

The black people who established Boley and the other black towns had clearly defined objectives. They were not necessarily anti-white, nor did they completely close themselves off from the mainstream of society. Many black people who came to the towns had been victims of slavery, southern oppression, and discrimination, and viewed a black community as a kind of protective shield. Total protection from racial prejudice proved impossible, but they did find a grand opportunity to share in the control of their lives and destinies. They could elect their own officials without harassment or pressure, establish committees, and speak openly without fear of reprisals from dissatisfied whites. Of much importance to them, they could avoid daily contact with those who considered black people inferior human beings. The future, however, brought trouble for the black towns. With the passage of time, they declined as young people left for cities within the state, or for those in the North and West. Opportunities also lured some of the town's older and more productive members. The magnet of the city had a powerful pull. Like other rural com-

Black wagon driver in front of Housel's Drugstore, Oklahoma City, 1889. Courtesy of the Oklahoma Historical Society.

munities, the decline of the all-black towns symbolized a broader movement in the United States, that of urbanization. The black towns did not offer a solution to the race problem, but they played an important role in the lives of their residents. They gave a sense of dignity and worth to their citizens and to many, that was enough to justify their existence.

Earning a living in prestatehood Oklahoma posed a challenge to blacks and whites no matter where they lived. Many made their living from farming or related businesses. During the era of slavery, blacks had often worked cotton and other crops; following the war many had engaged in subsistence farming. On the whole, agriculture never proved highly profitable for the black farmer who usually worked a relatively small holding compared to that of his white brethren. After statehood farm ownership among blacks, and the size of their farms, decreased sharply, thus making the economic plight of blacks even more difficult. But blacks vigorously pursued other occupations before 1907. A bustling black business community of-

The town council of Boley, Oklahoma. Courtesy of the Oklahoma Historical Society.

fered goods and services to citizens in such towns as Wagoner, Ardmore, Guthrie, Muskogee, Tulsa, and Oklahoma City. Blacks owned and operated gins, saloons (in Oklahoma Territory where they were legal), hotels, blacksmith shops, and a number of other businesses. A large number of black barbers did business in the territories and many never served fellow blacks. By and large, black business in the territories was small, but it fulfilled an important function in the black community. Cities with a significant black population had a small professional class, especially Muskogee, Guthrie, Oklahoma City, Ardmore, and Tulsa. In 1905 Ardmore could boast of a black professional group that included a lawyer, three medical doctors, a dentist, and a number of ministers and teachers.

The freedom from fear and the safety of citizens, whether businessmen, professionals, or farmers, depended upon effective law enforcement. Black troops had played an important role in policing unoccupied lands in Oklahoma and Indian territories. Black lawmen,

Green I. Currin, territorial legislator. Courtesy of the Oklahoma Historical Society.

like black soldiers, also contributed to life on the frontier and in Oklahoma. Among the most noted of these enforcers of the law, the names of Ike Rogers and Bass Reeves stood out, but perhaps a half-dozen others served as deputy marshals in the territories. Rogers earned much fame with his capture of the famous outlaw Cherokee Bill. Reeves had a reputation for a good mind and a quick gun, which enabled him to capture many a fugitive from justice. Despite their daring and creditable service, none of the black lawmen of the terri-

11

tories ever became a full United States marshal. And only recently have they won the recognition they rightly deserve.

Black men also assisted in making laws that governed the behavior of citizens in the territories. Some sat on Indian councils, and two served in the Oklahoma territorial legislature. In 1890 the people elected Green I. Currin of Kingfisher to the lower house of the legislature. A man of strength and much influence in fraternal circles, Currin enjoyed high standing in the black community, and within the white-dominated Republican party. As a legislator he tried hard to push through a civil rights bill, but that measure failed in the upper house. A second black lawmaker, D. J. Wallace of Guthrie, also won election to the lower house. He took his seat in 1893, and was a strong supporter of education. Like Currin he remained in the assembly only one term. Edward McCabe held the highest appointive position of any black during the territorial period, although a few blacks sat on various boards. After statehood the number who served in political positions dropped. From statehood to the mid-sixties only one black Oklahoman, Albert C. Hamlin, sat in the Oklahoma house and none in the senate.

The growth of social institutions among blacks accompanied settlement and political development in the territories. Religion exerted a most powerful influence among both young and old. Missionaries had arrived very early with the Indians and representatives of most of the major Protestant denominations worked among the blacks. Methodists and Baptists proved the most active. The churches of the territories showed concern for the general well-being of members, not just for their religious life. A few of the more progressive ones sponsored a variety of activities which included picnics, plays, family games, and other wholesome contests. Fraternal groups such as the Knights of Pythias, the Masons, and related women's groups, also provided socially healthy activities for black pioneers. From these groups the black community got some of its most distinguished leaders.

The schools of the territories provided limited social functions, but their major goal remained the education of the young. Following the war some of the tribes had provided for the education of blacks and the federal government and religious groups also assisted in their training. Oklahoma Territory created a public school system for blacks only a short time after its creation. Oklahoma City had a school in early 1891, and in 1892 Kingfisher had the first black high school. Some of these early schools had both black and white students. In

Jimmie Lewis Franklin

Left—E. P. McCabe. Courtesy of the Western History Collections, University of Oklahoma Library. Right—Bass Reeves, Deputy United States Marshal during the territorial period. Courtesy of the Western History Collections, University of Oklahoma Library.

1890, however, the territory adopted a policy of local option that permitted counties to segregate black and white students. Black parents tried unsuccessfully to defeat local option, and in 1897 the territorial legislature passed a stronger law that required the total segregation of black and white children. It also provided severe penalties for persons who violated the law. Although the measure required separation, a few black and white students probably attended mixed schools in the period after 1897. The passage of laws to segregate black and white children indicated what whites thought about race, and it also served notice of their future actions should Oklahoma and Indian territories become one state.

No public college or university existed in the territories for black students who wanted higher education until 1897. Faced with pressure from black leaders such as Edward McCabe, and with the possibility that a black student would demand admission to a white school, the Oklahoma territorial legislature created what was known as the Agricultural and Normal University, commonly called Langston University. The school was a land-grant college devoted primarily to the training of teachers. It prospered under its first president, Inman Page, who guided the school through its first seventeen years. Langston became an important educational and social institution, and its graduates rightfully took pride in a school that provided the state with teachers and other students who later acquired professional training out-of-state. Much of the state's black leadership came from the "school on the hill."

The desire to keep blacks and whites apart in the schools and colleges was an important commentary on race relations in the territories in the later part of the nineteenth century. In the period following the Civil War relations between blacks and whites were relatively easy. In fact, there was a rather close relationship between the two groups in churches, at social events, and in some public establishments. Many early pioneers could remember mixed schools and other institutions. One of them, Ben Randall, knew nothing about segregation. Blacks and whites sometimes served on juries, and one black settler could recall no hard feelings between the two races. This relationship, however, changed and near the end of the nineteenth century race relations became more restricted. And that was the case in many other parts of the country, especially in the South. During the period, the United States became more race-conscious and Supreme Court decisions, especially *Plessy* v. *Ferguson* (1896) did much to promote segregation.

Segregation and racial attitudes were of great concern to blacks when the people of the territories began to organize for statehood. In 1906 Congress passed the Enabling Act, permitting the people of the two territories to form a single state from Indian and Oklahoma territories. Blacks had to work long and hard to get Congress to include a provision that kept whites from taking away the vote. Specifically, the Enabling Act required that all citizens have the opportunity to vote without regard to color or previous condition of servitude. Blacks said this did not go far enough in banning discrimination, for they were very much aware of the growth of anti-black attitudes in the territories. The Equal Rights Association of Kingfisher, for example, charged that whites had no respect for black rights and regarded them as "niggers" no matter what their status. Unfortunately, the Enabling Act did not include all the provisions blacks desired and thus their fight against racism continued. Although dis-

Jimmie Lewis Franklin

appointed, they had little time to worry about their failure to get a stronger measure for the movement toward statehood was at hand. The Enabling Act had provided for a constitutional convention. Blacks wanted to assist in electing candidates who would support their struggle against segregation and discrimination in the new state. Politically, most of them were Republicans and they turned to that party for help. Throughout the campaign constitutional segregation stood out as a key issue. Many whites wanted to keep blacks apart in schools, on railroads, in waiting rooms, and in other public facilities. The Democratic party became closely identified with the effort to segregate. It pledged its support for white supremacy and it repeatedly cautioned against the mixing of the races which it said the Republicans would promote. To avoid Negro domination, whites should support the Democratic party. The appeal was clearly racist, but Democrats believed that only they could effectively fashion a good constitution for the new state.

In the election of delegates Democrats won all but twelve seats in the constitutional convention. It was a popular victory for the party and for the belief in white supremacy. Many thought that it had settled the so-called "Negro question." The election of Democrats, according to some observers, would surely make Oklahoma a white man's country. Clearly, it was a signal for the founding fathers of the new state to keep blacks segregated. In spite of the efforts of black leaders such as H. L. Storm and W. H. Twine, the editor of the Muskogee *Cimeter,* blacks and their friends had failed to defeat the supporters of Jim Crow—the believers in racial segregation. Blacks now turned to defeating the constitution if it contained objectionable provisions. W. H. Twine warned that he would wage a relentless effort to get President Theodore Roosevelt, a Republican, to veto any Jim Crow constitution.

It did not take very long for the convention to reveal its intentions. Led by its leader, William "Alfalfa Bill" Murray, who held strong anti-black views, the convention would have preferred to ignore the Enabling Act. Indeed, most delegates favored total segregation and wanted to enact a full Jim Crow program. But there was a serious problem. Would President Roosevelt and the Congress approve a document that restricted the rights of blacks? Few of the delegates at the convention wanted to take a chance on having statehood defeated. While the Jim Crow system was important to most of them, it was not as crucial, at that time, as the achievement of statehood. One delegate, C. N. Haskell, later Oklahoma's first governor, persuaded the convention to delay action on some racial measures until it had accomplished its major mission. Although Murray had desired swift and immediate action on the race question, he cleverly followed Haskell's advice and delayed the drive to completely segregate blacks and whites in the new state. The Oklahoma constitution did provide for segregated schools, gave the legislature the right to limit the franchise, and specified who was to be considered black.

Blacks waged an intense campaign to defeat what they regarded as a Jim Crow constitution. Protest groups in the territories, including the Protective League and the Afro-American League, sent representatives to Washington to urge the President to veto the constitution if the people in Oklahoma approved it. That group included notable black leaders Edward McCabe, A. G. W. Sango, J. Coody Johnson, William Harrison, and J. W. F. Sawner. To their regret the President had already decided not to stop the statehood movement. The people approved the constitution and also elected a legislature and a governor, Charles N. Haskell. Some citizens of the territories had desired stronger racial measures, and others had wanted separate statehood for Indian and Oklahoma territories, but they had not prevailed. Black people encountered despair but they again dug in for another intense fight to prevent the new state from erecting a Jim Crow system to limit their rights. They would fail. Their children, and their children's children would have to drink from the bitter cup of discrimination and segregation for many years to come.

Chapter 2

THE AGE OF SEGREGATION

The new government of Oklahoma moved swiftly to pass legislation to separate blacks and whites. Indeed the first bill that came before the Oklahoma Senate provided for Jim Crow in public transportation. Since territorial days a number of whites had pushed for such an act and proposals were presented to the territorial legislature but failed. The bill eventually passed by the first Oklahoma legislature required separate railway cars and waiting rooms for black and white passengers and provided a penalty for those who disobeyed the law. Subsequently, the legislature completed the "Jim Crow Code" with laws that prohibited marriage between blacks and whites, and which carried out the constitutional provision for separate schools. Most of the later restrictions upon blacks originated from custom. But in the period before World War II the state passed laws that segregated blacks and whites in public places including telephone booths, bathhouses, and mines. Jim Crowism became an important part of Oklahoma society, and remained undisturbed for almost a half century.

Whites regarded separate schools as an important cornerstone of Oklahoma's segregated society. Although whites spoke of "separate but equal" schools, few blacks believed the state would carry out the constitutional provision to maintain schools "impartially" for both races. Indeed, the allocation of money to the schools helped maintain a separate, inferior educational system for black children. Very simply, the state devised a plan which produced fewer dollars for black schools than for white ones. There was a noticeable difference in the outlay of funds for black children, and it resulted in poor facilities hardly adequate for producing well-qualified students. But a segregated system could not unduly concern itself with the development of top-flight minds for a black community many regarded as inferior. The comparatively poor state of black schools was obvious to honest and objective observers. Even a white administrator in the 1930s criticized the poor equipment and buildings black children had to use. The small amount of money that came from the county levy to support black education was altogether insufficient.

Few people in the history of Oklahoma worked harder than F. D. Moon to achieve better funding and quality education for black schools. Moon was born in 1896 in Fallis, Oklahoma, and attended Langston University where he received a Bachelor of Science degree. He held several teaching positions in Oklahoma before going to Douglass High School in Oklahoma City in 1940, where he served as principal for twenty-one years. Moon's active involvement in educational affairs and his efforts to insure fair treatment for black children and black teachers earned him the title "Dean of Black Educators" in Oklahoma.

Moon became president of the Oklahoma Association for Negro Teachers (OANT) in 1929, and for twelve years he served on that body's executive committee. Moon knew that the county levy was not adequate for the support of black schools, and tried to broaden the base of financial support. He also recognized that state law did not permit counties to issue bonds for building separate schools. During his first principalship at Crescent, Oklahoma, Moon had experienced the difficulties common to most rural black schools in the state—a lack of adequate supervisory personnel, ill-equipped buildings, insufficient funds for staff and for the development of good academic programs. Determined to master the serious problem of acquiring more funds for blacks, Moon contributed much time to the study of educational legislation. He persisted over the years, and in 1946 led a successful campaign to get a constitutional amendment to increase the building levy. Two years later he played a key role in the passage of another measure that raised the amount of money a county could allot for separate schools. These changes did not bring equality, but did strengthen education for black youths by adding millions of dollars to the budget of black schools. Teachers faced much difficulty in carrying out their tasks in the age of segregation, but they often achieved amazing results in spite of the limited support given them. They could thank F. D. Moon and other strong supporters of black education who made their tasks a little easier because of additional funds.

Emma L. Freeman also played an important role in changing the condition of black teachers and students in the state. In 1947 Freeman sued the Oklahoma City School Board for inequity in salaries

The integrated school of Mrs. D. C. Constant in the Seminole Nation, showing white, black, and Seminole children. Courtesy of the Oklahoma Historical Society.

between black and white teachers. Before her suit, the graduate of Kansas State Teachers College had taught twelve years in the school system, and she held a lifetime state teaching certificate. The attractive Douglass High School instructor and her attorney argued that she possessed the same qualifications as white teachers who performed identical work, but that her pay was lower. She asked a court to order the Oklahoma City School Board to equalize its pay scale. A federal district court decided to hear the case, but before it rendered a decision, Oklahoma City abolished its old pay system in favor of an equitable one. The judge of the court, however, did render a ruling to serve as a guide for the state. Oklahoma City, he said, had a duty to avoid any discrimination in salary because of race. The decision left segregated schools intact, but was a victory for the concept of equality of pay based on performance.

Black school officials, of course, continued to face restrictions because of limited funds. They could not experiment with the curriculum as freely as whites, and could not institute a broad range of extracurricular activities. Most black leaders, such as Moon, tried to offer a balanced curriculum. In line with the philosophy of the great black leader, Booker T. Washington, a number of Oklahoma schools established industrial arts courses. But on the whole, vocational education never assumed unusual significance in Oklahoma. Money from various philanthropic organizations greatly aided black educators in establishing some of these programs. Practically all of the large educational philanthropies gave money to black schools in Oklahoma. The Rosenwald Fund was important to Oklahoma, although several others made notable contributions. Rosenwald gave money for a variety of needs including libraries, books, transportation, and homes for teachers. The fund prompted the community to support education for its youth by insisting upon private donations before it offered a grant. Money from various funds could not overcome the effects of segregated education, but it did help to reduce significantly the amount of illiteracy in Oklahoma.

Blacks not only had to fight inequality in education but also an effort to disfranchise them. Many people viewed keeping the vote from black Oklahomans as another way to curtail their power and influence in government. For years black Oklahomans had been strong members of the Republican party. When Democrats took over the new state in 1907 and established a Jim Crow system, blacks stood more firmly by the party that had freed their people from slavery. Blacks' attachment to the party of Abraham Lincoln, and their opposition to the state constitution, however, angered Democrats and actually increased hostility among some of them. Thus Democrats did not find it hard to disfranchise them. When the Republicans showed signs of strength shortly after statehood, Democrats moved to limit the votes of black people.

The election of the first black, Albert C. Hamlin, to the Oklahoma legislature in 1908 also prompted the Democrats to act. A Republican, Hamlin came to Guthrie with his parents when he was only nine years of age. Before he reached age twenty he married Katie Weaver and became involved in a variety of local and civic activities. In the summer of 1908, he ran as a Republican candidate for the Third District in Logan County. Hamlin anticipated little problem in defeating his opponent, Teague Ray, since his district was mostly black and overwhelmingly Republican. With his defeat of Ray,

Dr. F. D. Moon (fourth from right), leading educator and president of the Oklahoma City School Board. Courtesy of the *Black Dispatch*.

Hamlin became the first black to sit in the state legislature of Oklahoma. Not until the election of E. Melvin Porter of Oklahoma City to the state senate in the mid-sixties would another black get elected to that body. Hamlin established a good record in the lower house of the legislature. He ran for re-election in 1910, but the growing strength of the Democratic party in the state helped to defeat him. His tenure in the legislature, however, brought justifiable pride to blacks.

There had been much discussion about the denial of the ballot to black people in the state before Hamlin's election. But the movement to disfranchise them now gained more momentum. In 1910 Oklahoma's first governor, Charles N. Haskell, called a special session of the legislature to devise legislation to limit the black vote.

21

The Blacks in Oklahoma

The legislature approved a measure that later went down in history as the grandfather clause. It provided that a person had to be able to read or write a section of the Oklahoma Constitution unless he (women did not yet have the vote) had antecedents who could vote as of January 1, 1866. The people had to ratify the amendment at an election. Blacks, Republicans, and members of the Socialist party, organized to defeat the measure. They said that it violated the Oklahoma Enabling Act and was an unconstitutional effort to rob black people of the ballot.

The people of Oklahoma approved the grandfather clause, although the black press had led a campaign to defeat the measure. No doubt the complicated method of voting on the measure aided its approval. Because some people did not understand that they had to cross out the words "For the Amendment," they may have voted for it. One thing, however, was certain; race played an important part in the election. And, not surprisingly, blacks and their supporters moved quickly to have the amendment overthrown in the courts. Black lawyers, A. G. W. Sango, J. Coody Johnson and others fought it in the courts for five years. Blacks tried to make their case by forcing registration officials to deny them a place on the voting rolls. The successful challenge came from Kingfisher. Here in the home of Green I. Currin, two registrars, Frank Guinn and J. J. Beal, attempted to keep blacks from voting under the grandfather clause. Convicted for violating a federal law, the men appealed their case to a federal circuit court and ultimately it reached the United States Supreme Court. In its decision, the Court ruled that the two had indeed conspired to prevent black citizens from exercising their political rights under the Fifteenth Amendment. It declared in *Guinn v. United States* (1915) that the grandfather clause was unconstitutional.

The state did not give up its attempt to keep blacks away from the polls. In 1916 Oklahoma turned to the passage of a literacy test to limit them. Governor Robert L. Williams strongly supported a literacy measure as he had the grandfather clause. After consulting legislators, he asked them to submit to the people an amendment which required of all voters an ability to read or write. Since this measure did not exempt anyone, Williams thought the court would not invalidate it. Everyone knew, however, the intent of the legislation. Thus, blacks labeled it the "second grandfather clause." J. B. A. Robertson, later a governor of the state, said that the measure would keep blacks out of Oklahoma. Democrats frankly declared that blacks should be disfranchised when that could be done "legally." Many

22

Albert C. Hamlin, first black legislator in the State of Oklahoma. Courtesy of the Oklahoma Historical Society.

whites, nevertheless, had reservations about the constitutionality of the new measure and did not want the state to go through another expensive court battle. Others felt that it would disfranchise too many white people. For those two major reasons, the people defeated the measure.

The final attempt to disfranchise black Oklahomans also came in 1916. At that time the Oklahoma legislature passed what was known as the Registration Law. It automatically qualified voters if they had voted in 1914, or if they had been *eligible* to vote in that year. Since the grandfather clause had not been invalidated by the Supreme Court until 1915, a large number of blacks, of course, were ineligible. The legislation's aim again appeared obvious. The law did not merely constitute a nuisance; it actually kept many blacks away from the polls. The fatal challenge to the registration law came in 1934. At that time I. W. Lane, mayor of the all-black town of Redbird, brought suit against county election officials for refusing to register him. In brief, he said that the registration law violated the Fourteenth and Fifteenth amendments to the United States Constitution. In 1939 the United States Supreme Court agreed. Black Oklahomans had won significant victories in their fight to maintain the ballot; and after the 1930s the state ceased making any effort to deny them the ballot.

The power blacks could wield was reduced for a time by limitations on the ballot, but economic restrictions also lessened their influence and the quality of their daily life. Of course, the Oklahoma constitution and state laws made no specific mention of the economic status of blacks. But the very logic that supported a Jim Crow society dictated the place they should occupy. It would have been unusual for blacks not to occupy the bottom rung of the economic ladder, for rarely was segregation divorced from discrimination in other areas of life. Whites understood very well that social progress and political power had always been closely tied to income, wealth, and financial status. Many of them wanted to keep blacks a race of small farmers, or in menial jobs which met the needs of the majority society. And for many years that was exactly the case.

Farming among blacks assumed great importance as a livelihood until mid-twentieth century. At statehood they owned considerable amounts of land, though most farms were small, and there was a significant difference in the value of black and white farms. By 1940, for example, white farms were three times as valuable as black farms. Most of these black farms, unlike those of the Deep South, were diversified and were not tied to a one-crop staple economy.

With each passing year both the number of farms and the total amount of acreage slipped. By the Great Depression of the thirties, the black farmer in Oklahoma faced serious problems. Active farm organizations could do little for him and his plight was as bad as that of his fellows in the Deep South. The hardship of the depression caused farmers to lose their best lands to banks who held mortgages on farms. In the decade of the thirties more than 37,000 Oklahoma blacks gave up farming. The decline was a symptom of what took place in other states of the South, but among white farmers the movement from the farm was not as striking. The shift away from the farm and declining farm ownership indicated the lessening importance of farming in the life of black Oklahomans. After 1940 every statistic suggested the waning significance of farming as an industry among blacks.

As blacks left the farm they tended to concentrate in the cities of the state, especially Oklahoma City and Tulsa, but many also settled in medium-sized towns. This movement had begun before statehood but the depression greatly accelerated the rush from the farm. By 1920 only a little over a third of Oklahoma's black population resided in urban areas, but twenty years later about 47 percent lived there. The plight of agriculture and the attraction of the city provided a "push-pull" force which continued the trend. By the decade of the seventies over 50 percent of the state's black population lived in Oklahoma's two large metropolitan areas, Oklahoma City and Tulsa.

The shift to the city affected how blacks earned a living but did not appreciably change their economic status. Jim Crow had been designed to reduce competition and that is exactly what happened. And as long as whites relegated blacks to menial tasks there existed no cause for friction. Occupationally, blacks who came to the city were concentrated in service, domestic, or laboring jobs. To whites, black subserviency in the city was as important as it had been on the farm. The occupations which experienced the greatest gains among blacks after the 1930s required little training and were the least profitable. Blacks from the farm came with great expectations of better wages and a good life. But black poverty resulted from the economic role assigned to them, and they simply exchanged rural for urban poverty. Only within the segregated black community did black workers acquire opportunities in occupations other than unskilled or domestic employment. In Tulsa, to cite just one example, the overwhelming majority of black men still held service jobs or worked as unskilled laborers as late as 1950. The same was true for Oklahoma City. Labor unions showed little interest in the plight of blacks, as was true for many white workers in a state which expressed hostility toward labor organizations until recent years. Not until the era of civil rights did any significant change take place in the occupational status of black Oklahomans, thus producing higher paying jobs and a sense of dignity and self-worth.

The system of segregation did provide jobs for black professionals who served the black community. The two largest groups were teachers and ministers, and as late as the seventies they still represented more than half the black professionals in the state. Medical doctors and dentists comprised the next largest groups, but there was a growing number of black lawyers in the state by mid-century. Segregation gave to the black professional a virtually protected market, but that represented a mixed blessing. If they profited economically by avoiding intense competition from their white counterparts, which was not always the case, they also suffered from being unable to practice their professions in the best institutions and in the best atmosphere. Doctors, for example, could not take advantage of the modern equipment and facilities at white hospitals. A few of them established small hospitals of their own, but they could not provide the service or the expensive equipment of larger institutions. Black lawyers had to endure prejudiced juries and harsh judges who could always threaten them with contempt of court. Faced with segregation and discrimination black professional groups such as teachers, lawyers, doctors, dentists, and undertakers very early organized their own state associations. Some of them still maintain separate organizations, but others have integrated.

Black businessmen, like black professionals, served a community created by Jim Crow. The foundation of black business had developed in the period before statehood and grew slowly following the state's admission to the Union. By and large black business remained small and reflected the economic condition of the black community. Blacks, however, organized establishments of many kinds to serve the black community. Dry cleaners, theatres, shoe shops, hotels, barbershops, nightclubs, and other businesses gave evidence of the initiative of black people. Many individual blacks succeeded. P. H. James and his wife founded a company in Oklahoma City which bottled an excellent soft drink called Jay Cola. They sold their product to both the black and white community, and earned a well-deserved reputation as efficient business people. W. C. Reed, a native of Muskogee, organized a small telephone system shortly after statehood and made a small fortune before he sold his business. A black company in Tulsa operated a bus line to serve the city's black population. In Oklahoma City the Universal Canning Company of E. D. Crowell did well with various products including spices and vinegars. Few black businessmen enjoyed more success or were as efficient as T. J. Elliott of Muskogee. Elliott's clothing store employed nearly thirty persons and handled thousands of dollars in merchandise during the course of a year.

The lives of two black businessmen offered a good picture of the success that sometimes came with ambition and hard work. The first, Walter J. Edwards, moved to Oklahoma City from Wellston in 1915 where he acquired a job at nine dollars a week. He later started a baggage company which he sold to purchase a carpet cleaning business. A man of great energy, Edwards built two service stations and bought a drugstore. The Great Depression hit him very hard, as it did other Americans. In the thirties he was broke, but junk saved him! Edwards acquired a small junkyard, but did not reap great profits until World War II. War created a tremendous demand for metal, and the price of scrap iron rose sharply. The Edwards' Scrap Iron and Junk Yard bought and sold millions of pounds of junk each year and in the process Edwards became one of the richest citizens in the state of Oklahoma. His business and money greatly aided the black community. Edwards had an interest in better housing for fellow blacks, and in 1936 he and his wife purchased more than thirty acres and built a housing addition that bears their name. In 1948 with the leadership of his wife, Frances, Edwards constructed a hospital in Oklahoma City. Built at a cost of $430,000, the 105-bed Edwards Memorial Hospital stood as one of the few in the entire South with a black staff. The institution remained open until 1966.

Sydney Lyons was also a businessman of great talents and organizational ability. Born in the Choctaw Nation, Lyons began his career in business in Guthrie where he operated a grocery store. Like Edwards, he eventually went to Oklahoma City where he founded the East India Toilet Goods and Manufacturing Company, which gained both a national and international reputation because of its quality products. Like Edwards, Lyons owned real estate, including farm lands. He also made money from the discovery of oil in Oklahoma City. Lyons built a park for blacks in Oklahoma City and gave to a number of worthy causes.

Lyons and Edwards were two notable examples of successful

black businessmen, but there were others. Jesse B. Blayton, Sr., a native of Garden City, Oklahoma, graduated from Langston and later achieved recognition as a teacher and as a practical businessman. A licensed Certified Public Accountant (CPA), Blayton was president of Atlanta's Mutual Federal Savings and Loan. George W. Davis of Muskogee took the leadership in organizing the Security Life Insurance Company in 1924. In 1930 this company was one of only sixty in the entire country. It had a racial appeal and from every indication fared well until the advent of the depression. Tulsan Ed Goodwin and his family engaged in several business ventures including the publication of the Oklahoma *Eagle.* Maurice Lee of Boley not only served as president of a bank, but invented a special process for barbecuing meat. By the seventies his sons were enjoying success from the sale of a barbecue appliance which sold under the brand name of Smokorama. Jake Simmons of Muskogee acquired wealth and influence through oil and real estate. Unfortunately, the resources of the black community were limited and there were not enough black businessmen and professional people to organize any large number of competitive financial institutions. For a time, however, two black banks existed in Boley, and teachers in some cities organized credit unions.

Black business benefited from the work of the National Negro Business League. Organized by the black leader Booker T. Washington, the league appeared in Oklahoma shortly after statehood. It grew until the post–World War II period when the Chamber of Commerce and other organizations began to compete with it. Much of the success of the early league came from the efforts of T. J. Elliott, the Muskogee businessman. He tried to generate a concern for opportunities available to blacks even in a segregated society, and endeavored to build their spirits in the face of hardships. He and others who followed him, particularly Roscoe Dungee, tried to point the black community toward cooperation and business diversity. Importantly, the Oklahoma Business League gave to the national organization one of its presidents, the incredibly gifted editor of the Oklahoma City *Black Dispatch,* Roscoe Dungee.

Black business operated in a community characterized by much poverty, a condition born of discrimination. The result of the economic plight of black people could be seen in many areas. There existed poor health conditions, high death rates, and a potential for crime and immorality. Poverty also helped to weaken the black family, and directly affected the development of black children. Jim Crowism made life a costly affair for the black community, and for society as a whole. Nothing mirrored the results of poverty better than poor housing. In the 1930s housing for blacks in the larger cities of Oklahoma left much to be desired, and living conditions were extremely bad. At mid-century the federal government still found over a third of black homes dilapidated. Many of them had neither running water nor private baths. Practically all of these homes were in totally segregated communities. Although the courts had legally outlawed segregated housing ordinances before 1950, in such cases as ex parte *Hawkins* (1936) and *Allen v. Oklahoma* (1936) the practice did not end, and no appreciable integration of housing took place until the 1960s and 1970s.

Racial beliefs that led to segregated housing and other forms of Jim Crow also promoted intolerance, and in some cases, outright violence. Keeping blacks "in their place" constituted a major objective for those who believed in racial inferiority. With legislation to support them, racial violence came easy to some whose sense of immorality was blurred by the need to keep blacks in an inferior position. Most whites, of course, did not condone open violence but many of them refused to speak out against injustice. During the first two decades of Oklahoma's history, lynching was the most open form of racial violence. Whites who participated in mob murder regarded it as an effective means of race control. Lynchings in Oklahoma usually followed a familiar pattern. They normally occurred before a crowd of white people who had an intense feeling of racial superiority and who felt "offended" by a particular act committed by a black. Mobs may have worked secretly to get their victims, but their murder was rarely quiet. A lynching took time, and it rarely became a hurried enterprise in Oklahoma. Death came to blacks by shooting, hanging, burning, or a combination of all three. White mobs in Oklahoma hanged most of their victims. Burning was the least used form of execution, but the most barbaric.

Few lynchings of blacks took place in the years before statehood. Whites in Indian and Oklahoma territories were more likely to become victims of mob violence than blacks. The early years of Oklahoma statehood saw an increase in the crime, although the *percentage* of blacks in the total population did not increase very sharply after 1900. It was significant that during the period of Oklahoma's greatest number of lynchings, 1910–1918, the percentage of blacks actually witnessed a *decline*. But whites believed that the number of blacks was increasing at a fast rate and this had an effect upon their behavior. The belief that blacks could dominate the state if not properly controlled did not alone account for brutal lynchings but that idea, coupled with fear of economic competition and the entrenchment of Jim Crowism, provided an atmosphere for violence by those willing to defy established rules of conduct.

Lynchings could produce fear, but they never stopped the attack upon discrimination and oppression. W. H. Twine, Roscoe Dungee, A. J. Smitherman, and other noted black newspapermen wrote bitter editorials against the barbarity of mob murder, and criticized law enforcement officers and the white leadership which tolerated murder. One black man considered it the religious duty of blacks to protect and defend themselves and their friends with guns if necessary. That was exactly what happened in one Oklahoma town when a group of blacks stole a car, armed themselves, and then stood guard over a prisoner until law officers spirited him away to safety. A. J. Smitherman of the Tulsa *Star* wrote that a mob respected strong, law-abiding citizens who acted.

The state of Oklahoma had a total of forty-one lynchings in its entire history. Just how many "near lynchings" occurred is impossible to determine. Interestingly, at the very time the crime was decreasing in the United States as a whole, it was increasing in Oklahoma. A number of groups and government officials, however, worked tirelessly to abolish mob murder. The most effective group in Oklahoma was the chapter of the Association of Southern Women for Prevention of Lynching. The women forcefully condemned murder and destroyed the argument about rape of white women as a major cause for lynching. They urged other whites to concentrate more upon black contributions and less upon alleged crimes of the race. Significantly, the state's governors took strong leadership in early Oklahoma in trying to stop lynchings. Their efforts, the work of the white women in the association and the determination of blacks not to be "bullied," brought a welcome end to lynchings by 1931. Lynchings, however, had brought unbelievable brutality and much embarrassment to a state eager to live down its frontier past.

During the 1920s the Ku Klux Klan carried out attacks against a number of Oklahoma citizens. Most of this violence was directed against whites, but blacks felt the lash of the Klan's whip, and its intolerance menaced the lives of many decent citizens. The black press, especially the *Black Dispatch* and the Muskogee *Cimeter* warned the Klan that the black community would not bow to intimidation by cowards who paraded under sheets. Klan lawlessness was

Mt. Zion Baptist Church on fire during the Tulsa race riot, June 1921. Courtesy of Mrs. Ruth Avery.

greatest in the Tulsa area. When conditions worsened in that county and elsewhere in the state in 1923, Governor Jack Walton sent troops to restore law and order. He pledged to stamp out mob rule and violence in Oklahoma if he had to place every county under military law. Walton's eagerness to smash the Klan, which had become a political force in the state, led him to extremes, and even some of the governor's supporters turned against him. He became engaged in a serious fight with the legislature, which Walton viewed as Klan controlled, that proved his undoing. The legislature impeached him. Klan violence soon decreased, and the organization never again became a significant political factor in the Sooner State. It revived during the civil rights movement of the sixties, but more as a small social irritant than anything else. The efforts of citizens' groups and law enforcement officials, and the cooperative endeavors of blacks and whites helped to effectively reduce racial tensions in the state.

The most deplorable incident of racial violence in the history of Oklahoma took place in Tulsa, in 1921. Tulsa had a population in excess of 100,000, but was a rapidly changing town. A city on the move, some of its citizens sought profits through illegal means as the law looked the other way at crime. It contained 10,000 black

The destruction on "Stand Pipe Hill," after the Tulsa race riot, June 1921.

people, representing more than 12 percent of the population, a much larger percentage than most cities in the state. Blacks, much like whites, had come to Tulsa in search of profits and with the hope of advancement. Many had left the South where they had confronted harsh conditions. They were determined people, hardy and aggressive, with an understanding of democracy, justice, and fair play.

Riots, like wars, never have a simple cause. It is not hard, however, to discover the most important reasons for the terrible disaster at Tulsa. On the last day in May 1921, a white elevator operator accused a young black man, Richard Rowland, of attempting to rape her. When the woman screamed Rowland fled, probably aware that the woman's action had endangered his life. Later, he said that he had accidentally touched the woman's arm as he boarded the elevator. Rowland doubtless knew that a charge of rape by a white woman against a black man was a serious affair. To those who understood Oklahoma history, Rowland's flight did not imply his guilt. It simply meant that he was afraid. Before 1921, several Oklahoma blacks had met death by shooting and burning for alleged rape. After Tulsa officials arrested Rowland they placed him in a secure jail. An inaccurate newspaper story then stirred emotion in the city. In a poorly researched account, the Tulsa *Tribune* reported that Rowland had attacked an "orphaned" white girl, Sarah Page, and that the accused had admitted putting his hand upon her. Contrary to the paper's reporting, Rowland had not torn Page's dress and

Courtesy of Mrs. Ruth Avery.

scratched her face and hands. The *Tribune* story displayed terrible journalism, and it directly contributed to the ugly disaster that followed.

Anger and emotion gripped the white Tulsa community when it learned what had allegedly happened to the white woman. The *Tribune* story had fueled the fires of hatred. When the sheriff of Tulsa County heard of a possible attempt to lynch Rowland, he took action to secure his safety. Later, however, a group of armed white men appeared in the downtown area of Tulsa in the vicinity of the jail. Black men of Tulsa who had long been accustomed to protecting their rights decided that they would not permit the lynching of any black man in the "Oil City." A number of them acquired automobiles, armed themselves and went to insure Rowland against harm, and to protect his right under law to a trial by jury. Police ordered blacks to disperse, to return to their homes in "Little Africa," as some called the black section of Tulsa. Before they heeded that request, shooting broke out between the black and white groups. Several people died in the clash, and more would die in the days to come.

Whites moved to teach blacks a "lesson," to put them "in their place." They successfully pushed them from the downtown area, back to "Little Africa." At first many whites were satisfied in keeping blacks contained within the black section. But for unexplained reasons, probably sheer mob psychology, the white attack became more aggressive. Many in the mob now wanted to "invade" the black community to "burn the niggers out." And that they did! Black people did not yield submissively, and fought back to defend their homes from lawless white mobs.

Killing and destruction in Tulsa eventually prompted Governor J. B. A. Robertson to call out the Oklahoma National Guard. By that time, however, much damage had already been done and more than a score of people had lost their lives. Many blacks had been shot and killed in a ruthless manner and before the holocaust ended, a total of thirty-six people were officially listed as dead, but the figure was probably much higher. There was really no accurate way to account for all those who had been burned to death, dumped in rivers, or buried in undisclosed places, especially if the murdered persons had no family or close friends. And there was also so much despair and disappointment some Tulsans probably did not bother to register the death of some loved ones.

Many of Tulsa's most noted black institutions lay in ruins. A. J. Smitherman's Tulsa *Star,* champion of black manhood and equality, met the torch, and so did the Oklahoma *Sun.* The Howard Cavers, business leaders in the community, lost all they had worked to attain. White arsonists reduced elaborate and beautiful Mount Zion Church to ashes. An $84,000 building, one of the most beautiful in the Southwest, had literally gone up in smoke. Tulsa's black community rebuilt it, but it took years for many citizens to get back on their feet. Some never did. The story of Mt. Zion is a remarkable commentary on confidence and will. But it was only one of many which came out of the "Tragedy of '21."

The riot embarrassed Tulsa, but the city did not change its social policy or abandon discrimination. The riot did not greatly alter race relations in Tulsa. Tulsa had assisted blacks who needed help, or who found it necessary to resettle, but it hardly had the choice short of permitting many of them to wander the streets in search of shelter and food. That, of course, would have been a threat to the general society which white Tulsans surely did not desire. But Tulsa was not a very penitent community, and as official documents reveal, it forgave the lawlessness of the white mobs who killed and burned. Most whites believed that the riot had really been caused by lower-class blacks who were "worked up" by white agitators for social equality, and by Communists. It was easy to believe what one wanted to believe. A Tulsa grand jury report placed the blame for the riot squarely upon the shoulders of the black men who went downtown to defend Rowland. It ignored the rumors of a lynching by whites, and accused the blacks of threatening the public interest. The report also noted that doctrines of social equality had much to do with the "Tulsa War of 1921."

Racial violence in Oklahoma was not divorced from the political and social system. A system of race relations made racial inferiority and separation important ingredients in the minds and lives of white Oklahomans. And rabid defenders of the system could easily excuse emotionalism and, on some occasions, bestiality, by believing that they were in effect *acting for the state* while they engaged in violent acts.

The National Association for the Advancement of Colored People (NAACP) waged a continuing battle against violence and discrimination in Oklahoma. A group of blacks and whites founded the organization in 1909, and it came to Oklahoma four years later. The idea for a branch of the association in Oklahoma originated with Henry A. Berry who taught at Douglass High School, and who also sold the *Crisis* magazine, official publication of the NAACP. Anxious to defend the rights of black people against Jim Crow and to end humiliation, he investigated means for the establishment of a local branch of the NAACP in Oklahoma. Berry consulted the principal of his high school, J. H. A. Brazelton, and they later called a conference to meet in Avery Chapel Methodist Church in Oklahoma City. They laid plans for a local chapter. In June 1913, when much unrest existed in Oklahoma over the persistent efforts to fasten second-class citizenship upon blacks, the first NAACP chapter in Oklahoma came into being. The initial chapter contained twenty-eight members who chose Dr. A. Baxter Whitby as the organization's president. The branch encountered some difficult years, especially during the World War I period when there was a slowdown of activity. The Oklahoma City chapter was reorganized in 1918 at the Calvary Baptist Church. At that time it began to take on new life, a fact attributable in great part to the efforts of the *Black Dispatch* and Roscoe Dungee.

No individual played a greater role in the development of the NAACP in Oklahoma and in the progress of civil rights than Roscoe Dungee. Like his father, a minister, he believed in race pride. In 1915 Dungee began publication of the *Black Dispatch* which preached equality, and which for over fifty years under his editorship played a major role in the fight for social justice. Dungee's involvement, however, was not narrow. He served as president of the National Negro Business League. He sat as a member of the National Board of the NAACP and as a member of the Executive Council of the Association for the Study of Negro Life and History. His life touched practically every facet of black existence over a long career and few constructive civic, political, or social movements escaped his attention or support. His most striking achievement was the organization of what became known as the State Conference of Branches of the NAACP. The conference idea was his brainchild and he worked hard in selling it to the national office. The conference plan—a group of local chapters organized on a state level for a common goal—enabled state groups to have more latitude in bringing civil rights suits. As a consequence the Oklahoma NAACP, in conjunction with the national office, became one of the country's most active branches.

Dungee had many natural talents, but his dedication to civil rights accounted for his respect in the black community. The editor symbolized strength and hope for blacks, and they were often emboldened by his fight for their rights. Whites may not have appreciated Dungee's criticism of Jim Crow society but they had to respect his honesty and his intellectual abilities. They found it difficult to argue against his contention that a moral democracy demanded fair play for all people regardless of color. Dungee troubled the white mind. Whites, however, could not attack him for un-Americanism for he was a great believer in America and American institutions. With Dungee as a firm supporter, the NAACP scored a number of victories in Oklahoma. In the 1915 *Guinn* case the Supreme Court ruled against the grandfather clause, the first major victory for that organization. The Oklahoma chapter showed aggressiveness and on appeal it carried other cases to the high tribunal. Before the decade of the forties, the two most important decisions beside *Guinn* were *Lane v. Wilson* (1939) and *Hollins v. Oklahoma* (1935). In the *Lane* case, the court outlawed a law which attempted to further restrict black voting after the grandfather clause had been overthrown. In the *Hollins* decision the United States Supreme Court reviewed the conviction of a black man accused of raping a white woman with whom he allegedly had a secret affair. As a result of the court's action, Hollins's life was spared, although he later died in prison. The NAACP achieved some of its most significant triumphs in the 1940s and 1950s in decisions involving education. Much of its success was due to Dungee and his close workers in the organization such as Amos Hall of Tulsa and Jimmy Stewart of Oklahoma City. The NAACP tried to defeat racism through legal means and education. In the early part of the century, whites looked upon the organization as militant, and many of its members met harassment, economic pressure, and in some instances

Roscoe Dungee, newspaper editor and civil rights leader. Courtesy of the Oklahoma Historical Society.

physical abuse.

Blacks within the NAACP believed that they had the right to all the advantages which America and Oklahoma had to offer. Some black Oklahomans thought they could never defeat racism and decided to leave the land they had desperately tried to love. Even prior to statehood there had been a Back-to-Africa movement. Indeed in the very year following the organization of the NAACP in Oklahoma, the state witnessed one of the country's most celebrated Back-to-Africa schemes. The movement was led by a man named "Chief Alfred Sam," a complex character many regarded as devious. Sam came to Oklahoma six years after statehood and began to sell shares in an organization he called the Akin Trading Company. When a person purchased stock in Sam's company, he received a "free" trip to Africa. For a small number of blacks who had tired of the state's attempt to make them second-class citizens, the Chief's offer was inviting. It seemed an excellent opportunity to get a new start in the "motherland." Here was hope for them, for their children, and for generations yet unborn. Having recruited perhaps a hundred blacks from eastern Oklahoma, Sam delivered about sixty of them to the Gold Coast of Africa. But the Chief experienced economic failure. Faced with poverty and disappointment, the blacks sought aid to return home to the Jim Crow and discrimination they had supposedly left behind forever.

The Back-to-Africa movement has real importance in the history of black Oklahoma. Sam understood that a dissatisfaction existed which caused many blacks to despair of ever gaining full recognition and opportunity in Oklahoma. He also fostered a sense of race pride. To some, nevertheless, Sam was nothing more than a deadbeat, a fraud who tried to exploit black people. No other Back-to-Africa scheme ever made headway in Oklahoma. In the 1920s at the height of Marcus Garvey's Back-to-Africa movement, most of the black leadership in the state proved hostile toward Garvey's Universal Negro Improvement Association (UNIA), especially Roscoe Dungee. Blacks in Oklahoma accepted America as their home and they were not willing to say good-by and good riddance to a land they had helped build.

Despite severe restraints the black community developed a vigorous social and cultural life during the age of segregation. Among the most significant social institutions was the black church. The church enjoyed a growth in membership following statehood. Baptists were most active, and in 1906, the group formed a state organization, the Oklahoma Baptist State Convention. By statehood the total number of black church members stood at 26,000; and by 1940 this figure had jumped to 80,000. Baptists claimed 57,000 of that number, and they continued to reflect great strength in future years. The state, of course, had a variety of denominations which came to include the Black Muslims in the years of the sixties. Blacks desirous of praising the Lord had little difficulty finding a house of worship. There were many—too many—some contended. In 1936, to cite just one statistic, the state had over 770 churches, nearly 500 of them Baptist. In Oklahoma City alone there were more than fifty-three churches at the time, and Tulsa had about the same number. White Methodists had almost three times the number of members as blacks in the late thirties, but blacks had about half the number of buildings that their fellow churchmen had. The abundance of churches was not healthy for the black church because it created a contest for funds in a community already suffering from poverty.

The black church in the state of Oklahoma did more than preach about hell and heaven. It was far more active in social affairs than in many other states. It did preach a rather conservative theology, but it did not keep its head buried in the sand. Long before the 1960s there had been clergymen who believed that the church not only had a direct responsibility to care for the poor and the sick, but to fight social injustice and racial hate in the world. Some of the state's black churches offered community service programs which provided wholesome recreational, educational, and other social activities. Musical events, athletic contests, and club work gave both young and old an opportunity to free themselves from the everyday cares of life. As a young man growing up in Oklahoma City, Ralph Ellison, the distinguished novelist, read books in the library at Avery Chapel Methodist Church. In that same city Quayle Memorial Methodist Church organized Bethlehem Center in 1946 which not only provided a social outlet for young people, but served as a training ground for future leaders.

The black church and the black clergy could not live divorced from the reality of segregation and discrimination. Before the era of the 1960s, when black churches played a strong role in the fight against injustice, black ministers and their congregations had preached against the evils of oppression. They maintained that the church had an obligation to work for democracy and justice within society. In the opinion of many black churchmen the church had to serve as a vehicle of hope for the black community. It had to insure that society did not become unresponsive and uncaring. Black ministers reminded the white church of its failure to work for black freedom and against racial injustice. Black ministerial alliances in such cities as Chickasha, Tulsa, Oklahoma City, and Muskogee in the years prior to the so-called civil rights revolution boldly confronted the issue of segregation, and attacked the shallowness of a Christian faith which permitted the denial of human justice.

The Reverend E. W. Perry was a remarkable example of a black minister whose religious and social work inspired the black community. Perhaps no minister in the history of black Oklahoma has ever acquired as much power as this Baptist clergyman. And he used much of his influence to attack injustice. As the pastor of Tabernacle Baptist Church in Oklahoma City, he became the denomination's leader in Oklahoma, and for more than forty-two years he headed the Oklahoma Baptist Convention. He was also an important figure in the National Baptist Convention. Perry was a bitter opponent of segregation. In 1920 when a group of white ministers invited him to speak at one of their gatherings, he seized upon the opportunity to lecture them on their Christian responsibilities. He reminded them that the blood of Christ flowed through the veins of both blacks and whites. And although he disavowed social equality, which many whites mistook for forced social mixing, he told his fellow preachers not to spend time worrying about white supremacy but to think more of the brotherhood of man. Perry, of course, was merely one of a number of black ministers in Oklahoma who preached a doctrine spoken more forcefully by blacks in the era of the black revolution. From the 1950s through the 1970s black ministers and the church would play a leading role in helping to break down the walls of segregation and discrimination. In fact, it would be difficult to contemplate a civil rights movement in Oklahoma, or the American South, without thinking of the black preacher and the black church.

The church gave the black community both a religious and a social outlet. Other institutions, however, sponsored important social and cultural functions. Fraternal groups, important since territorial days, continued to attract much interest. Some of them such as the Masons had an exceptionally large following. The Knights of Pythias, the Elks, the Odd Fellows, and other groups had devoted followers. These organizations and associated women's clubs sponsored many events for the black community, as some of them had during the territorial period, and they also assisted in self-help programs. They held public dances, supported youth affairs, established funds for the poor, and worked for recreational projects. Many noted black leaders in Oklahoma, including Roscoe Dungee, attorneys Amos T. Hall and E. Melvin Porter, and civic leader Jimmy Stewart, came from the ranks of fraternal organizations. But they were only four of a large number of outstanding personalities.

By the second decade of statehood the black Oklahoma community had available to it a variety of inexpensive social entertainment and intellectual activity. Blacks enjoyed the presentations of touring road shows and the concerts of national celebrities who performed in the larger cities of the state. Young people took advantage of the scouting movement which appeared in the early years of statehood. And after World War II the Young Men's and Young Women's Christian Association strengthened their programs which provided for wholesome recreation for black youths. In the decade after the 1920s the radio and the "picture show" furnished moments of delightful relaxation to those who wished to escape from work or from daily routine. Only television, after mid-century, would overtake radio and the movies as the most popular form of entertainment. Because of the efforts of Judith Horton, blacks could take advantage of a small number of public libraries across the state. Excluded from the white library in Guthrie, Horton organized the Excelsior Library in 1908, the first public library for blacks in Oklahoma.

Special events and athletic contests gave blacks an opportunity to relax and enjoy themselves. Local towns often organized baseball teams. In the larger cities such as Tulsa and Oklahoma City, blacks could see professional baseball players who came to Oklahoma during the era of the professional black leagues. In the years before integration, rodeos and state fairs experienced popularity with blacks. J. Coody Johnson organized the first state fair with the objective of promoting agriculture and livestock raising among the state's rural black inhabitants. He also wanted to encourage healthy competition among them.

Few participants provided as much excitement for blacks at a rodeo as William "Bill" Pickett, the famous black cowboy. Pickett invented steer wrestling, or bulldogging, as it is commonly called. He grew up in Texas, but later joined the 101 Ranch Wild West Show in Oklahoma. Pickett originated the sport of bulldogging when he rode alongside the animal, jumped on its back, clenched his strong teeth into the animal's lip, and then flipped it over! Billed in rodeo events as the Dusky Demon, he bulldogged more than 5,000 cattle before his tragic and untimely death. Pickett gave more to rodeo than any other cowboy. One of his most spectacular—and most dangerous—performances came at Sand Springs, Oklahoma in 1920. Pickett failed to throw his animal the first time and the angry steer plowed up the ground with his head. Blood covered his face and an attendant had to bandage it so that only his eyes were visible. Gallantly, the black cowboy re-entered the arena and threw his steer, to the delight of the crowd which showered him with coins. Had not the color line restricted Pickett, he would have been a contestant

Bill Pickett, "bulldogger" and member of the National Cowboy Hall of Fame. Courtesy of the Oklahoma Historical Society.

at many other rodeos between 1910 and 1930. In 1932 Pickett lost his life when a horse kicked him in the head. For his contributions he earned a place in the Cowboy Hall of Fame in Oklahoma City in 1971, the first black to receive such recognition.

Black women in Oklahoma made an important contribution to the black community through the organization of social clubs. In 1906 the women of Guthrie had formed the Excelsior Club, and in April 1910, a call went out for a meeting of a state organization. The in-

Rubye Hall, member of the Oklahoma State Regents for Higher Education since 1974, and chairman 1978–79, with Governor David Hall. Courtesy of the *Black Dispatch*.

strumental force behind the organization of the Oklahoma State Federation of Colored Women's Clubs was the woman who became its first president, Harriet Jacobson. Mrs. Jacobson came to Oklahoma from Kansas, and for some forty years she was connected with public schools in Oklahoma. She was also an officer in the Oklahoma Association of Negro Teachers and served through the terms of several of its administrations. Mrs. Jacobson organized the Eastside Culture Club of Oklahoma City, the initiator of the movement for a state federation. Under her leadership the state group worked hard for legislation which established a training school for boys at Boley and a girls' training school at Taft. A number of distinguished women followed Mrs. Jacobson in the presidency of the federation, including Judith Horton, the second president and founder of Excelsior Library at Guthrie. The clubs of the federation, and the ones outside of it, sponsored a wide range of activities which touched almost every segment of society. Some of them gave scholarships and loans to black students, worked for civic improvement and strongly supported civil rights activities. Although a variety of functions later competed for women's attention in the modern era, women such as Eunice Simmons and Rubye Hall, former chairman of the Oklahoma State Regents for Higher Education, worked long and hard to keep the club movement alive in Oklahoma.

Music and musicians occupied a central place in the social life of the black community. In Oklahoma City, Zelia Breaux trained many young and eventually famous musicians in her music courses in the Oklahoma City schools during her long career. The cities of the state gave the nation many of its best performers. Idabel proudly claimed organist Earl Grant, while Muskogee gave birth to many nationally recognized personalities including among them Don Byas and Jay McShann. Tulsa produced Earl Bostic and Ernie Fields. Enid gave the world opera star Leona Mitchell who began her singing career in churches, but who later thrilled audiences in the United States and foreign countries.

Oklahoma City was the home of two of the nation's most gifted and most renowned musicians, Charlie Christian and Jimmy Rushing. Christian came from a musical family and began to play the guitar very early. In the late thirties the brother-in-law of the famous bandleader Benny Goodman discovered Christian who was then playing in a small Oklahoma City nightclub. Goodman hired him, and he was headed for New York City and fame. He mingled with the great and near-great, but in the early 1940s he contracted a serious disease and doctors had to place him under special care. In 1942 he died of pneumonia, still in his twenties. Serious jazz artists remember Christian as a master, and many of them still appreciate his "Solo Flight." Rushing, like Christian, had a musical background. He received much inspiration from his father and from his teacher, Zelia Breaux, under whom he learned to read music. He left Oklahoma City as a young man but returned to join a local band. He later played with the famous Benny Moten Orchestra in Kansas City where he became one on the country's greatest jazz singers. When he left Moten he went with the famous Count Basie Band where he remained until he formed his own group. Rushing is best remembered for his piece "Mr. Five by Five."

Oklahoma's capital city also served as headquarters for the Blue Devils. This dance band produced an impressive number of talented musicians, including the great Jimmy Rushing. But others stood out: Harry Youngblood, Oran "Hot Lips" Page, Willie Lewis, and Buster Smith. For a short time the band also included William "Count" Basie before his rise to prominence. Organized in 1923 the Blue

The great guitarist Charlie Christian. From *Applause*, Vol. II, No. 3 (1945), p. 55.

Devils made their home in the Ritz Ballroom, but the band traveled widely within Oklahoma, and to cities in nearby states. The Blue Devils' favorite city was Kansas City, the jazz mecca of the Midwest, and also the home of a man named Bennie Moten who assisted a number of black musicians toward national fame. The Blue Devils fared well until the onset of the depression, which made survival difficult. There was little money for entertainment; so the clock began to run out on the Devils. Larger bands which had more popularity began to raid the group and quickly some of its more talented members began to defect—Rushing, Page, Smith, and Basie.

The presence of a vigorous social life did not imply blacks' contentment with their status within Oklahoma society. State and local laws and customs forced black people to develop and maintain their own institutions. Segregation kept blacks and whites apart in social settings. That racial separation helped to foster a sense of insecurity that came with living in a society which constantly reminded blacks of their "inferior" status. Yet, the system of segregation never succeeded completely in defeating the pride which black people had, and it never shattered a healthy black identity. Later that pride and that identity would confront the long-standing practice of racial separation and discrimination in a bitter fight for justice. Justice would win out.

Chapter 3
FAREWELL TO AN OLD ORDER

As Oklahoma approached mid-century, the state's black community comprised some 145,000 souls. In 1890 the number of blacks had stood at 22,000, but it jumped in excess of 137,000 within a twenty-year period. During the next two decades the black population continued to increase but not at the same dramatic pace, and not at the same rate as the total population. At the opening of the 1930s there were 172,000 blacks, but the number declined between that time and 1960. Gradually, however, the black population climbed back toward the 1930 figure. The highest proportion of blacks in the total population since statehood was registered in 1910 when it stood above 8 percent. It has not surprised some experts that the growth of the black community has been relatively slow in recent years. As early as 1940 a study of the black community's population predicted little chance of significant growth. It stressed that the low birth rate and the large number of infant deaths would tend to keep the black population small in Oklahoma. It is interesting to observe that the percentage of blacks in the state's population in 1979 was smaller than in 1940 although the absolute number of blacks was larger.

The black population became increasingly urban, but that fact alone had no profound effect upon the structure of segregation until the cities became the nucleus for civil rights activity in the 1950s and 1960s. The depression of the 1930s greatly accelerated the move to the city and toward urban as opposed to rural employment. In 1920 only about a third of the state's blacks lived in urban areas, but by 1940 this figure had climbed to 47 percent. The city sustained its attraction and projected hope, so that by the seventies over half of Oklahoma's black community lived in the state's two largest metropolitan areas, Tulsa and Oklahoma City. Few blacks lived in western Oklahoma. The concentration of blacks in the cities had not only political and social effects, but also helped create an atmosphere for change that ultimately spelled the demise of segregation.

Black people, even as rural inhabitants, had never been passive toward the system which kept them from enjoying the benefits of full citizenship. In the early years after statehood, to place the issue of desegregation in focus, blacks were not as concerned about "integration" as they were about "equality." But they opposed enforced segregation for they knew that inequality came along with it. Blacks achieved some limited success in acquiring full citizenship rights, but by the decade of the forties, Oklahoma, like other states of the South, remained segregated.

The World War II era brought changes to the state and to the entire nation. The war forced the United States to expend money, and to sacrifice men, to defeat a racist German government which killed millions of Jews. Americans had the opportunity to witness what hatred could achieve when a nation made it a fundamental part of its program. And black soldiers, many of them Oklahomans, made important contributions to victory over the Nazis and their allies. After the war it was hard for whites to ignore their role as dedicated patriots. Blacks received support from white reformers who believed that America had not lived up to its promises to its largest minority. Perhaps the most searching study of the relationship between the treatment of blacks and the ideal of democratic government came in 1944 with the publication of Gunnar Myrdal's classic, *An American Dilemma*. That book had an impact upon postwar developments in civil rights, and it helped to shape a more positive attitude on race in America.

Segregation, however, seemed almost indestructible to many citizens. They could not foresee that the walls which kept the old system in place would come tumbling down so quickly. The first major assault upon Jim Crow and discrimination in the period after the war came in the field of higher education. The condition of Langston did much to prompt the attack. Although it was the only black school in the state, its progress had not been rapid, and it had been insufficiently funded. Unquestionably, Langston produced both outstanding leaders and citizens, but it encountered difficulty in carrying out a first-class academic program and extracurricular activities. Yet, it achieved a great deal of success which belied the amount of support it received from the state. Not only did Langston attract a committed faculty but it had one of the best athletic programs in the nation for a school of its size. Its most noted athlete before the era of integration was Marcus Haynes, basketball star of the Harlem Globetrotters, but the school produced other young men whose only obstacle to professionalism was their blackness.

Clearly, Langston did not compare favorably with the other institutions of higher learning in Oklahoma. The school had neither advanced nor professional degrees for young black students, but programs existed for white youths at more than forty-three institutions on the eve of desegregation. The scarcity of programs and the limited availability of subjects had much meaning within the context of segregation. The lack of courses of study and available facilities at Langston suggested to blacks that it was unnecessary or not advisable for them to train in certain professional fields or disciplines. Many white Oklahomans did not relish the idea of pouring large amounts of money into an institution to train blacks for fields where they would compete with whites. Others simply did not believe in preparing blacks for anything except teacher education and agriculture.

Before 1948 blacks who desired degrees or courses not offered by Langston went out of state for them. Much like other southern states, Oklahoma paid a portion of the expenses of qualified blacks who studied for their degrees elsewhere. Legislators designed the program, in part, to avoid any possible legal attack on segregation. Oklahoma, they reasoned, could argue that it was in fact providing equality of educational opportunity. Begun in 1935, out-of-state grants supported nearly 2,000 students before integration made the program unnecessary. Actually, the state policy made education expensive for black students since many of them had to travel far from home to attend school. Moreover, the grants rarely ever covered any significant percentage of the costs incurred by a student. Throughout the history of the program, the Oklahoma legislature did not appropriate more than $50,000 a year; and grants usually averaged only about $140 per student. The program was a striking denial of equal educational opportunity. It also added a burden upon institutions within the community (especially churches) that often had to contribute money to those students who went beyond Oklahoma for training.

The inequality of higher education in Oklahoma invited direct legal opposition by blacks. In 1946 a young black woman named Ada Lois Sipuel applied for entrance to the University of Oklahoma Law School. Even some of the strongest defenders of segregation had anticipated a court battle long before Sipuel requested admission to the school at Norman. They had pointed out that insufficient funding of Langston would spell trouble unless the legislature changed its policy. Others stressed that the lack of certain programs at the black school endangered the system of separate education. In the opinion of many blacks and some whites, Langston should have received a much larger percentage of the money appropriated for higher education. As the law required, the University of Oklahoma refused Sipuel admission. The president of the university, George L. Cross, stated specifically at the request of the NAACP, that race was the reason for not accepting the young Chickasha native. Sipuel's attorney, Amos T. Hall of Tulsa, went to court to seek admission to the school for his young client, arguing that the Fourteenth Amendment dictated equal educational opportunity. The Cleveland County District Court decided for the university and against Sipuel. On appeal the Oklahoma Supreme Court refused to reverse the lower court, but Hall and Thurgood Marshall, chief counsel of the NAACP, did not become discouraged. Marshall had been one of the architects of the legal assault upon segregation and was prepared for the intense battle that lay ahead. Segregation, he consistently proclaimed, meant illegal discrimination, and what many termed separate but equal was nothing less than judicial myth. His argument, of course, had not been convincing enough for the Oklahoma court which stated its obligation to uphold the law as long as it did not conflict with the United States Constitution.

No one expected Sipuel to abandon her fight. She appealed the case to the United States Supreme Court. Simply put, her attorneys argued that Oklahoma was in violation of previous decisions issued by the court, especially *Missouri* ex rel. *Gaines v. Canada* (1938), which said that states must provide equal educational facilities. In January 1948, the Supreme Court reversed the Oklahoma court. While it turned to *Gaines* in its decision, it did not consider the constitutional issue of segregation. It merely stated that the Fourteenth Amendment did in fact guarantee equal educational opportunity; and for Sipuel, that meant a legal education in a state school. But the Court did not require the admission of the black student to the Law School at Norman. State officials were unhappy over the ruling but applauded the Court's decision not to deal with the broad issue of segregation, or to order Sipuel's admission to the white university. In an attempt to protect its system of separate higher education the state created the Langston University School of Law in Oklahoma City. Truly, it was a law school in name only. Roscoe Dungee, who had been involved in the case from the beginning,

Ada Lois Sipuel Fisher, a principal in the integration struggle at the University of Oklahoma. Courtesy of the Oklahoma Publishing Company.

quipped that the state had tried, although unsuccessfully, to pull off a miracle by establishing a first-class law school overnight. It was clear to almost everyone that the state was trying to circumvent the court decision to provide equal education within the state of Oklahoma. The NAACP and Sipuel's attorneys noted that if Langston could not offer equal educational opportunity since it did not have accreditation, then surely its new law school could not award a degree of any quality. Sipuel would have nothing to do with the new Langston Law School, and renewed her request for admission to the University of Oklahoma Law School. Again she failed; but a series of events helped to bring her success, and end a long era in Oklahoma history.

By the beginning of 1948 the NAACP had already devised other plans to topple segregation in higher education in Oklahoma. In a clever maneuver, the organization developed a strategy to counter obstacles devised by the state. The NAACP recognized that Oklahoma could not possibly establish enough professional schools for any significant number of students who wanted to take degrees in several fields. Under the Supreme Court's decree the state had an obligation to provide substantially equal educational facilities. Thus, in the spring of 1948 the NAACP had six black students apply for admission to the University of Oklahoma to pursue courses unavailable at Langston. How could the state meet this new crisis without expending thousands of dollars? President Cross, as had been the case with Sipuel, rejected the applications. Oklahoma found itself in a terrible bind.

One of the six students denied admission by Cross quickly brought suit against the university. His name was G. W. McLaurin, a native of Oklahoma City who had come to the state sixteen years before statehood. At the time of his suit, McLaurin was on the faculty of Langston University. The state contended in its defense before the court that the fifty-four-year-old college professor had been rejected because of race and in accordance with state law. In the summer of 1948 a federal district court ordered the state to give the black professor the courses he requested. But the court again refused to touch Oklahoma's segregation laws. The McLaurin decision "shook up" state officials for it was the first time in the history of Oklahoma that many of them could foresee a possible end to segregated higher education.

McLaurin entered the University of Oklahoma under the court's decree— *on a segregated basis.* To keep him apart from other stu-

Jimmie Lewis Franklin

dents the university prepared special seating, giving the student his own "exclusive" section in places around the campus. McLaurin found the special arrangements for him aggravating and demeaning. Thurgood Marshall, his attorney, characterized them as stupid, and fought to remove the indignity to McLaurin. Enforced segregation of McLaurin within the University of Oklahoma, said Marshall, constituted a badge of inferiority; thus it was illegal under the United States Constitution. McLaurin's attorneys asked a federal court to restrain the university from segregating him. Keeping him separate from other students, they contended, negatively affected his relationships with them and his professors. Moreover, they said that isolating the black student had a detrimental effect upon his study and concentration. A lower federal court rejected the request. The decision read much like the old 1896 *Plessy* ruling which had legally established segregation. The court stated in June 1950, that the Fourteenth Amendment did not abolish distinctions based on color or race, and that it was not designed to enforce what the court called social equality between the races. On appeal, the United States Supreme Court reversed the lower court decision. It ruled unanimously that McLaurin's segregation restricted his rights and that the University of Oklahoma was in violation of the Fourteenth Amendment. McLaurin, said the judges, was entitled to the same treatment as any other student. *McLaurin v. Oklahoma State Regents for Higher Education* (1950) was a strong blow to the separate but equal doctrine.

In the meantime the state had resolved the Sipuel problem and that of the other students. By late 1949, the state had wearied of the attempt to fight off desegregation. Educational officials had spent countless hours attending to detail, and the attorney general had devoted a large amount of time to the integration controversy. Accordingly, the Oklahoma legislature changed its laws so that black students were permitted to enroll at universities in the state. Ada Lois Sipuel (Fisher) was one of those who entered, three years after her initial suit. Much like McLaurin, the students who attended the Norman campus had been segregated, in some cases roped off, until the court issued its 1950 decision which outlawed the practice. The long struggle over desegregation in education had come to an end, but other problems remained.

The various federal court decisions which related to higher education in Oklahoma brought hope to blacks that the public schools could not long stay separate. Among those who believed in segregation there was genuine cause for concern. Concern became alarm

53

for some in 1954 when the United States Supreme Court issued its famous *Brown* v. *Board of Education of Topeka, Kansas,* ruling which declared segregated education inherently unequal. But panic did not overtake most Oklahomans. Many had anticipated the decision. Moreover, the state had become conditioned to controversy, and the hard battle over integration at the University of Oklahoma had "sapped" the energies of a great many citizens. Of much importance was the statesmanlike leadership of politicians such as Governor Johnston Murray and his successor Raymond Gary. Gary made plain his intention to abide by the law, and he cautioned against overreaction and violence.

Oklahoma moved quickly to implement the *Brown* decision. State officials urged school boards to act responsibly, and admitted openly that *Brown* was here to stay. The legislature responded to the decision by giving attention to the way the state financed education. Lawmakers had little doubt that the method of financing the separate schools would not meet a stern test in court. Consequently, they moved to dismantle the system of separate levies for black and white schools by the passage of a constitutional amendment, commonly called the Better Schools Amendment. Some opposition appeared when the legislature referred the measure to the people for approval. Opponents said that it would spell the end to segregated education. White supporters argued that the state needed the amendment in case the federal government insisted upon implementing the *Brown* decision. Governor Gary strongly supported the proposal. A man of deep religious convictions, the governor did not see integration as an end to the world, or to civilization in Oklahoma. When the people passed the Better Schools Amendment in April 1955, Oklahoma had taken an important first step toward reshaping the past and creating a more positive image of itself.

Oklahoma began public school desegregation in 1955 but some private schools had begun a year earlier. In reality the opponents of the Better Schools Amendment had been correct—the measure did make it more difficult to maintain separate schools. As expected, little violence occurred in Oklahoma, though many problems complicated integration. Both blacks and whites found themselves involved in a process which was totally new and which had been illegal for half a century! If some discomfort and suspicion characterized the behavior of both groups, history could serve as a good explanation. Fundamental problems plagued blacks, such as the dismissal of teachers and the development of a spirit of cooperation among those with whom they did work. Some blacks also found that formerly all-black schools had been important cultural centers for them, but were now less so under integration. And that disturbed many of them. Nevertheless, Oklahoma had made a good start. Integration was indeed established.

Just one year after the famous *Brown* decision an event occurred that changed the course of southern history and the history of blacks in Oklahoma, the Montgomery bus boycott. It marked the emergence of one of the country's most noted leaders, Martin Luther King, Jr. King, a Baptist minister, believed in nonviolent direct action and civil disobedience to overthrow unjust laws. The son of a clergyman, King held a Ph.D. degree but he had much appeal to the common man. He possessed charisma, a special trait of personality which proves attractive and which helps to persuade people. Blacks responded to King's teachings. To accept an unjust system passively, he taught, was to cooperate with evil; thereby the oppressed became as evil as the oppressor. Noncooperation with evil was a moral obligation, and cooperation with good, a necessity. The oppressed, King told his followers, should not allow the conscience of the oppressor to slumber. To tolerate injustice told the oppressor that his actions were morally right. King, however, rejected violence no matter how difficult the circumstances, and made it clear that nonviolent resistance was directed at *oppression,* not at oppressors. King created a powerful movement to free black people and his personality proved so commanding, and his leadership so visible, that the period in black history from 1955 to 1968 may well be called "The Age of King."

Blacks in Oklahoma made wide use of the sit-in, a nonviolent tactic, in their march toward first-class citizenship. The leader of the sit-in movement in Oklahoma was an energetic, highly vocal woman named Clara Luper, Director of the Oklahoma City NAACP Youth Council. A native of Okfuskee County, Luper took her undergraduate degree at Langston University, later received a master's degree from the University of Oklahoma, and has been a teacher for many years in the state. Luper believed in democratic government and her training as a social studies specialist doubtless had some impact on how she viewed America's failure to solve the race problem. Prior to her involvement with the sit-in movement, she had been active in civil rights. Discrimination, she contended, degraded blacks, and amounted to immorality. A believer in King's philosophy of nonviolence, Luper set out to overthrow segregation in public places. She knew that legal methods took too much time and had often failed. Therefore, she turned to a technique that would bring the difference in treatment of blacks in public places to the attention of the entire community, and which would create such inconvenience that injustice to blacks would end. She targeted Oklahoma City for protest.

Like other cities in many parts of America, Oklahoma City and other municipalities in the state adhered to a policy of segregation. There was much logic in striking at Oklahoma City; it had the state's largest population and it was the capital, the center of political power. And it provided Luper with a potentially large number of young black youths to man her "children's army" against segregation, bigotry, and injustice. A strategic victory in Oklahoma City, she correctly reasoned, would have an important effect upon other parts of the state, and any success would help to condition the white community for even greater changes. After much preparation Luper and her NAACP Youth Council were ready to act.

When white eating establishments failed upon request to change their policy of segregation, Luper struck at downtown stores in Oklahoma City. In August 1958, the Youth Council conducted a "sit and wait" demonstration against Katz Drugstore. The thirteen original participants in this historic event in Oklahoma ranged from six to sixteen years of age. Luper had taught them well about nonviolence and about their major mission. Whites experienced shock when the well-dressed young blacks took their seats and requested food to eat *within* the establishment, not "to take out," as had often been the custom in many businesses which were segregated. Some whites became angry when the children persisted in their demonstration against Katz, but after days of protest the drugstore changed its policy. Within the next year a few other stores gave blacks service, including the S. H. Kress Company. Much hard-core resistance, nevertheless, remained. Luper intensified her attack with greater media coverage of the sit-in, and as a national movement placed more emphasis on civil rights activity. Moreover, as young blacks saw their friends express their bravery by sitting at a counter, or standing in a picket line, they became more inclined to "do something for freedom." Fired by the example of Oklahoma City, demonstrations took place in a few other Oklahoma cities. Clara Luper had been right about the success and impact of a sit-in in the state's capital.

Victory came slowly in Oklahoma City and did not arrive completely until the mid-sixties. Restaurants such as Anna Maude's and Bishop's waged a strong battle but they, too, eventually fell. The support of many whites, especially within the religious community, had a positive effect upon the sit-in movement. Clergymen such as Father Robert McDole not only condemned discrimination in public accommodations, but also actively participated in civil rights demonstrations. McDole saw the separation of the races as one of the major moral issues which faced America and he preached that the existence of racism threatened democracy in America. Blacks greatly profited from the support of such men, and they became increasingly certain that they would be "Free by '63." As the echo of "Freedom Now" reverberated across Oklahoma, it seemed for the first time in the state's history that Jim Crow could totally collapse.

By the mid-sixties black protesters in Oklahoma and other parts of the country had broadened their attack to include not only eating places (which had often been the initial target), but other public accommodations. Entertainment centers, hotels, libraries, parks, and a host of other establishments came under attack. Springlake and Wedgewood amusement parks in Oklahoma City exemplified the hard-core opposition to integration which blacks often encountered. The manager of a Lawton amusement park said that he would never accept business from blacks. The owners of white businesses argued that integration would hurt their income, that whites would not support them if they permitted blacks to use the facilities. The issue to them was not a moral one, only financial. Obviously, they could not understand the argument of black protesters that human rights were more important than property rights. Blacks maintained that they had a right to buy food in a restaurant, to rent a hotel room, or to purchase entertainment without any consideration of race. It was a moral consideration; and it went to the heart of their quest for justice.

A series of fast-moving national and local events brought success to blacks. At the time blacks began the sit-in movement in Oklahoma, the NAACP had formulated an ordinance written by Dr. F. D. Moon which called for desegregation of public accommodations in Oklahoma City. But in 1962 the city still did not have such a measure; thus, black leaders and their followers decided upon an unyielding campaign to bring about passage of a public accommodations law. They were not content to rely upon the goodwill of businesses to open their doors, and to keep them open. To be sure, a number of establishments had abandoned past policy but the NAACP and other groups such as the Congress of Racial Equality (CORE) wanted to get the principle of equality written into law. That, alone, they said, would insure the proper behavior of both business people and white citizens. They also knew that a great number of blacks who had grown up under the old system would not frequent newly integrated places without the protection of law.

The passage of a national civil rights bill would accomplish the objectives for which blacks had worked. Following the election of President John F. Kennedy in 1960, the pace of the civil rights movement quickened. The young executive's firm commitment to racial equality pleased blacks, as did his party's endorsement of public demonstrations. Indeed, Kennedy was the first American president to openly condemn segregation as a moral wrong. Freedom-rides, sit-ins, and other forms of protest documented rising black anger and impatience. To render a final blow to racial discrimination and to highlight the need for employment opportunities for blacks, a number of organizations decided to stage a "March on Washington." In August 1963, an estimated 200,000 black and white Americans converged on the capital to "send a message to the Congress." To this gathering Martin Luther King, Jr. delivered his now famous "I Have A Dream" speech which captured the mood of the civil rights movement, and which so eloquently expressed the goals for which blacks worked. Within three months of this massive march President Kennedy was assassinated. His death and the elevation of Vice President Lyndon B. Johnson to the presidency gave impetus to the drive for a civil rights bill. A Texan, Johnson had overcome a great deal of the provincialism which could have easily kept him from acting in the best interest of blacks and the country. He had a powerful black movement on his hands; he moved decisively, urging the Congress to act in a manner which would have pleased the slain Kennedy. Southerners and a few northern conservatives tried to kill the bill, but failed. Congress triumphantly passed the 1964 civil rights measure and Johnson signed it. Among other things, it outlawed discrimination in most public accommodations. Enjoyment of the bill's benefits, of course, rested upon strong enforcement. Some white Americans, particularly in the Deep South, had hoped that fear would keep blacks "in their place" and away from white establishments. Black leaders recognized the necessity of breaking any remaining fears and of challenging the federal government to take action against those who disobeyed the law. They also realized that a number of pro-integration whites silently welcomed the effort to ensure enforcement. If those whites continued to do business at establishments which integrated, that could serve as a powerful lesson to the white community. A few businessmen even quietly applauded the law and the effort to test it, because that relieved them of the risk of voluntarily opening up their doors.

A sit-in demonstration in Oklahoma City. Courtesy of the Oklahoma Publishing Company.

No notably violent confrontations took place during the early application of the civil rights law in Oklahoma. The fact that some cities had already integrated their establishments doubtless had some effect in keeping peace. A number of citizens feared that trouble would come in Little Dixie. The state's governor at the time, Henry Bellmon, urged citizens to be law-abiding, although they may have disagreed with the law. He later traveled to southeastern Oklahoma to determine the mood of the people. Suspicion about the willingness of Oklahomans in Little Dixie to honor the law caused the members of the Oklahoma City Chapter of CORE to take a trip to that section of the state to test the act. According to CORE's leader, Archibald Hill, the people in Little Dixie were not predisposed toward obedience to the new civil rights law, and he claimed that had not his followers had protection, violence would have resulted. But violence did not take place; and the state's human rights director, William Rose, accused CORE of exaggeration, and of giving a one-sided picture of what transpired. The absence of violence, of course, did not mean that the people of southeastern Oklahoma or any other section had altered their attitudes overnight. Clearly, this was not the case. Discrimination had been in place for many years, and it would take more than a federal law to produce fundamental changes in attitudes. Importantly, however, the statute had changed white's behavior, and that in itself had much merit.

With the acquisition of more rights and with rising expectations, the mood of blacks in Oklahoma and in other parts of the country began to shift. The passage of the civil rights measure had left much yet undone and it remained an urgent matter for some to complete the task of freedom. Was it not true that '63 had passed, and full freedom had not yet been realized? The fall of each obstacle seemed to refuel the fires of freedom. Even before the passage of the civil rights bill, black leaders in Oklahoma had formulated a plan that included the abolition of discrimination in practically all areas of life. Not until 1968, however, would the state pass a statute which supplemented the 1964 federal law which wiped out discrimination.

By the end of 1966 the civil rights movement had taken on a more militant complexion. One heard much of "Black Power," a phrase first used by a young black leader, Stokley Carmichael, of the Student Non-Violent Coordinating Committee (SNCC, pronounced Snick). Carmichael was a brilliant and highly articulate student from Howard University. He had firsthand knowledge of the South and had seen the brutality of racism close up. Carmichael parted from

King's philosophy of nonviolence. Because he spoke of possible retaliation, many people readily associated Black Power with violence. Few could define the term very accurately, and even a book by the originator of the phrase did not help very much. Whatever it was, Black Power caught the imagination of large numbers of black youths on campuses across the country. And it was here that Carmichael found persons sentimentally attracted to his rhetoric. With the death of King in 1968, nonviolence suffered a terrible blow, and in the wake of his dastardly murder, riots again occurred in major cities across the country. Violence—and the very talk of violence—had a dramatic effect upon the civil rights movement. It divorced many old-line organizations from the newer ones headed by more youthful blacks who spoke of the "black revolution," and the "liberation struggle." Violence had a fragmenting effect within the black community. There was, too, a change in mood regarding integration. One black Oklahoman now questioned the whole idea of "mixing." Why, he asked, would blacks choose to "integrate with people who despised them?" A growing spirit of black nationalism surfaced in some quarters although it never appeared very pronounced in the state of Oklahoma. Perhaps one of the most notable results of the change in mood was the creation of a heavily black civil rights movement.

The rhetoric of Black Power was more noticeable in Oklahoma than outright violent militancy. The NAACP, the Urban League, and groups such as Jimmy Stewart's Oklahomans for Progress, never lost control of the civil rights movement in the state. They had much more rhetoric; they had the power, the influence, the resources, and the know-how. And importantly, they had a consciousness of history which had enabled them to fight continuously for many years. But Black Power's rhetoric, especially on the national level, may have had some important effects. Some older black leaders used the threat of violence to urge whites to cooperate in bringing about peaceful change. Real progress could undercut militancy, they advised. The mood created by Black Power probably prompted many citizens to take a closer look at the causes that excited many blacks to take to the streets, and others to lash out violently in frustration against Jim Crow and discrimination. More than any other time in American history, blacks expressed their deeply felt anger to whites in no uncertain terms. A usually moderate Tulsa minister, for example, accused some whites of uncivilized behavior and he labeled his city and state racist.

A consciousness of blackness and a sense of racial pride grew with the success of the civil rights movement. Perhaps the most en-

61

during legacy of black militancy was the idea of an aggressive, united black community, a kind of brotherhood and sisterhood of blackness, although militancy in many instances proved disruptive. What was defined as "soul," that sometimes indefinable quality associated with black life, became the hallmark of a people who had lived out the experience of oppression. Soul food and innumerable soul affairs appeared in the Oklahoma community. Beauty pageants, talent shows, black art exhibitions, and dramatic productions increased as the phrase "Black is Beautiful" became popular among those who sported their sense of racial pride. When the beautiful Coretta Banks of Lawton took part in the Miss Oklahoma Pageant in 1970, blacks could smile, testimony in itself that far-reaching changes had taken place in Soonerland.

The revitalized emphasis on race pride coexisted with the much broader movement to integrate Oklahoma society. Black students, the soul of the Freedom Movement, pressed to get into colleges and universities, and once there, they fought for the recruitment of more black students and black faculty. Since the mid-fifties when Prentice Gautt joined the University of Oklahoma football team, the state's universities had turned out some of the finest black athletes in the country. Black students appreciated the efforts of these institutions, but encouraged school administrators to broaden recruitment to include nonathletes. Some of the black students' strongest demands involved the necessity for an expanded curriculum. They argued that the contributions of black Americans had been ignored, and that universities should establish courses which told of their efforts. Black student groups insisted upon a more active role in the life of the university, and called for greater participation on committees that determined their future. They also requested more funds for extracurricular activities and cultural programs. As a result the state's universities were able to invite to their campuses a number of black creative artists, scholars, politicians, and social activists who often brought a healthy, and sometimes radically different point of view from that of many students who had grown up in provincial surroundings.

The strong concern about black life and culture in the early 1970s led to a greater interest in the works of three of Oklahoma's most distinguished intellectuals: novelist Ralph Ellison, poet Melvin B. Tolson, and historian John Hope Franklin. All three had achieved distinction before the 1960s but the black revolution made their names common in most intellectual circles and among many people who otherwise would have ignored them. Each possessed enormous talents and their legitimacy as creative artists and intellectuals rests upon their ability to think, to write, and to render a valuable service to society. Their professional and critical acclaim has had less to do with the fact that each often treated black themes than with their colleagues' respect for their work.

Ralph Ellison is one of America's most gifted writers. A native of Oklahoma City and a graduate of Douglass High School, Ellison grew up during the early years of Jim Crow in the new state. He never doubted his worth, and discrimination never succeeded in creating in him a sense of inferiority. As a boy, young Ellison read widely, and often slipped away quietly to find a book at Avery Chapel Methodist Church where his mother worked. Before he was ten, Ellison had already read some of the best writers of literature. Upon leaving Oklahoma City and Douglass High School, he went to Tuskegee Institute in Alabama. He wanted to become a musician, but he soon experienced a change of mind.

Apparently Tuskegee made a profound impression on young Ellison although a lack of money forced him to leave the school founded by Booker T. Washington. He went to New York where he met the great black novelist Richard Wright who gave him his first opportunity to publish a short story. Ellison began to take writing very seriously. Although he left New York briefly, he returned to work with the Federal Writers' Project which provided him a bare subsistence. Near the end of World War II he joined the Merchant Marine. In his judgment it offered many more opportunities for blacks than the army or other branches of the military and there was not the miserable Jim Crow. His choice shaped his future, for much of his later fame rested upon that decision. In the Merchant Marine Ellison received encouragement to write a novel.

Ellison's book, *Invisible Man* (1952), is a masterful work that deals with the question of racial identity and the problem of surviving in a modern and very complex world. The major character, a black southerner, tries to find meaning for his life, and that search finally pushes him North, away from a college environment which, incidentally, reminds one of Tuskegee during the era of Booker T. Washington. In the North he discovers that his industry and self-reliance do not bring him recognition—the identity he craved. In the eyes of whites he still had no visibility. Finally, he is forced to live underground, but by then he has resolved that even a person who was "invisible" had a socially responsible role to play in American society.

Ellison's brilliant novel is in many ways a powerful commentary on American culture, and had it not exploited a racial theme, it probably would have still gained much acclaim. Critics applauded its literary execution and technical precision. The book won a number of awards including the National Book Award and the Russwurm Award. Since its publication Ellison has combined teaching with writing. Recently, Oklahoma City honored its native son by naming a library in his honor; and the Oklahoma legislature also recognized his contributions to American literature.

Melvin Tolson's rise to fame came slowly. He grew up in the state of Missouri and studied at Lincoln, Fisk, and Columbia universities. It was at Langston, however, that Tolson made some of his greatest contributions, although he had given distinguished service at other places before he joined the school in Oklahoma. Some critics see Tolson as one who constantly challenged the old order and those who lent it support. Practically all of them agree that perhaps his real gift to American poetry was his ability to combine profound intellectual ideas with "ham hocks, ribs, and jowls." Tolson could relate well to those who had lived a particular kind of experience, especially in the South. The lines below are an excellent example of his ability to capture the meaning of blackness in the South and in America.

> I was born in Bitchville, Lousyana.
>   A son of Ham, I had to scram!
> I was born in Bitchville, Lousyana;
>   so I ain't worth a T.B. damn!

and

> I came to Lenox Avenue.
>   Poor Boy Blue! Poor Boy Blue!
> I came to Lenox Avenue,
>   but I find up here a Bitchville, too!

or

> I want some ham hocks, ribs, and jowls,
>   a pot of cabbage and greens;
> some hoecakes, jam, and buttermilk,
>   a platter of pork and beans!*

---

*From *Harlem Gallery* (Reprint. London: Collier-Macmillan, 1969), 73, 75, copyrighted by Twayne Publishers and reprinted here with the permission of Twayne, a Division of G. K. Hall and Company, Boston.

Jimmie Lewis Franklin

In 1940 Tolson won the National Poetry Prize for his poem "Dark Symphony." Some of his most familiar and often-quoted lines are from this piece. Many young black reformers and writers of the 1950s and 1960s found "Dark Symphony" a meaningful commentary on black life in America. It scolded the country for keeping blacks oppressed and expressed the hope that justice would prevail, and that black people would triumph over democratic evils. "Dark Symphony" skillfully registered the pulse of black America, and constituted a bitter indictment of a Jim Crow system that gave the country an ugly image and which stifled the development of a people. There was little symbolism and few "far out" lines in Tolson's verses below:

They tell us to forget
The Golgotha we tread . . .
We who are scourged with hate,
A price upon our head.

They who have shackled us
Require of us a song,
They who have wasted us
Bid us condone the wrong.

They tell us to forget
Democracy is spurned.
They tell us to forget
The Bill of Rights is burned.

Three hundred years we slaved,
We slave and suffer yet:
Though flesh and bone rebel,
They tell us to forget!

Oh, how can we forget
Our human rights denied?
Oh, how can we forget
Our manhood crucified?

When Justice is profaned
And plea with curse is met,
When Freedom's gates are barred.
Oh, how can we forget?*

*The verses from "Dark Symphony" are from *Rendezvous With America* (New York: Dodd, Mead and Company, 1944), 38–39, and appear with the permission of Dodd, Mead and Company.

It took many years for the Langston poet to "move up from the back row," and he was understandably disappointed that his fellow professionals so long ignored his creations. Before his death, however, such writers as Allen Tate and Karl Shapiro had critically praised Tolson's work. Liberia honored him as its poet laureate. Increasingly, editors of books in American literature have turned for selections to the poet's major works, *Rendezvous with America* and *Harlem Gallery* for selections.

Historian John Hope Franklin has earned both national and international recognition as a teacher and scholar. Born the son of a Rentiesville attorney, young Franklin had also anticipated a career in law. Like Ellison, who grew up in the very same period of Oklahoma history, Franklin had a change of mind. After he left Tulsa's Booker T. Washington High School, he went to Fisk in Nashville, Tennessee, where he excelled as an undergraduate student. At Fisk he developed a love for history, and decided to pursue graduate studies. The depression of the thirties brought hardship and diminished the hope of obtaining a higher degree at Harvard. Fortunately, Franklin had won the respect of one of his Fisk professors, Theodore Currier, who signed a $500 bank note, thus enabling the future historian to fulfill his ambitions.

A good literary style and careful research have made John Hope Franklin one of the most widely read historians. He has authored many books and scores of articles and reviews. His highly acclaimed history of blacks in America, *From Slavery to Freedom,* was published in 1947, and has gone through four editions. It is the leading text in the field of black history and reviewers have praised it for its broad coverage, its accuracy, and objectivity. His other works have generally met with the same appraisal. His penetrating book, *Reconstruction; After the Civil War* has had a significant impact upon how historians look at that subject, and it may be Franklin's best study.

Franklin has taught and lectured at some of the finest institutions of higher learning. He served on the faculty at Fisk, St. Augustine College, North Carolina College at Durham, and Howard University. For an eight-year period from 1956 to 1964, he chaired the history department at Brooklyn College. From 1967 to 1970 he headed the department at the University of Chicago where he presently holds the John Matthews Manly Distinguished Service Professorship. Franklin has also taught abroad at the Saltzburg Seminar in American History in Austria, and has been a Fulbright Professor at several foreign universities. In 1962 he went to England where he served as

John Hope Franklin, historian and member of the Oklahoma Hall of Fame. Courtesy of the Office of Public Information, the University of Chicago.

Pitt Professor of American History at Cambridge University.

Franklin's dedication and his excellence in scholarship have been recognized by his colleagues. He has been president of the American Studies Association, the Southern Historical Association, and the Organization of American Historians. In 1978 members of the American Historical Association elected him president of that organization. Thus he is the only person in American history to hold the presidencies of all four of these major professional groups. When his alma mater, Fisk University, announced that it would establish a chair in his honor, John Hope Franklin became the first black American ever honored in such a manner. The state of Oklahoma paid its respects by inducting the historian into its Hall of Fame in 1978. When Fisk University saluted its famous graduate with a John Hope Franklin Celebration Dinner in March of 1979, it exalted not only the honoree, but it also recaptured a heritage that went back to Oklahoma. Dr. Gloria B. Jackson has paid justifiable tribute to the scholar from the small, all-black town of Rentiesville in her poem "Hope Is His Middle Name."

> Hope is his middle name.
> From the plains of Oklahoma he came.
> To Fisk University with a fire.
> For education he had a desire.
> As a scholar he had no peer.
> His motives were always clear.
> To learn, to write, to teach.
> No knowledge was beyond his reach.
> The search for his people's story.
> Destined him for fame and glory.
>
> Hope is his middle name.
> From the plains of Oklahoma he came. *

The careers of Franklin, Tolson, and Ellison as intellectuals are testimony to individual achievement, and to their own abilities to overcome the restraints imposed by a now outmoded social system. The change created by desegregation has now significantly broad-

---

*Dr. Gloria Jackson's poem is printed on the outer cover of the program prepared for the John Hope Franklin Celebration Dinner held in Chicago, March 10, 1979. Copy in the author's possession. Used by permission of Dr. Jackson.

ened and strengthened intellectual and cultural life among black Oklahomans. The limitations that once confined the activities of many gifted black artists have disappeared. Young black Oklahomans can now look forward to practicing their crafts without the disadvantage occasioned by color. The renewed emphasis on black life and culture which accompanied the civil rights movement in the late sixties and seventies further sparked greater concern for fine arts festivals and for the dramatic arts. The greatest achievement in the dramatic arts came with the organization in Oklahoma City of the Black Liberated Arts Center (BLAC). Led by George Wesley, BLAC encouraged participation in dramatic productions, and its influence was felt throughout the state by the activities it sponsored. Before his affiliation with BLAC, Wesley had been associated with WKY-TV in Oklahoma City which produced the Emmy Award winning documentary, "Through the Looking Glass Darkly" that told the story of black Oklahomans.

The period of the sixties also brought about changes in black political life. The most significant result was the reappearance of blacks in state politics from which they had been absent for more than half a century. When legislative reapportionment came as a result of a court decree, blacks insisted upon some legislative districts which would virtually insure them representation. They achieved success. In the state election following reapportionment black legislators were elected from Oklahoma and Tulsa counties. John White and Archibald Hill came to the house from Oklahoma County, while Curtis Lawson represented Tulsa. The state's lone black senator was an Oklahoma City attorney, E. Melvin Porter. Each of these legislators had engaged in the struggle to better life for black people in Oklahoma, but they did not have to depend solely upon their civil rights record for their election to office. Of the four black lawmakers three were attorneys and one (White) worked in insurance. Since their election the largest number of blacks to serve in the state legislature at any one time has been five. All eight who have been elected were Democrats, and all have come from Oklahoma and Tulsa counties. With few exceptions they were middle-class, highly ambitious, and well educated.

The only black woman ever to serve in the state legislature has been Hannah D. Atkins. She has been one of that body's most effective lawmakers. A native of North Carolina, Atkins took her undergraduate degree at St. Augustine College. She also holds a library science degree from the University of Chicago. Married to Charles N.

Atkins, the first black to sit on the Oklahoma City Council, she has received numerous awards and much recognition for her work. She has been active within the Democratic party, serving on the party's National Committee, and has supported literally scores of civic activities. She is one of the most active legislators in the house or senate. Atkins is gracious, well educated, and a highly articulate woman with a pleasing personality. She has avoided tunnel vision and she has worked diligently for a variety of legislative issues, including women's rights and mental health. Atkins may have the best opportunity of any black to compete successfully for the governorship of Oklahoma or a United States Senate seat.

Since the return of Oklahoma blacks to state politics, attorney E. Melvin Porter has been the only black elected to the state senate. Porter is a skilled politician who likes combat and, some contend, controversy. A native of Okmulgee, he left Oklahoma to attend Tennessee State University, and took a law degree at Vanderbilt. Upon his return to the state he supported a number of causes, and soon rose to leadership in the civil rights movement. Blessed with great ability as a speaker, and with a sharp and agile mind, Porter vowed to fight racism. He aligned himself with the Oklahoma City branch of the NAACP and eventually became its president, a position he kept until going to the state senate.

Despite bitter attacks and opposition from some quarters, Porter has remained in the senate for fifteen years. He appears unshakable and some say unbeatable. He rarely shies away from a bitter political battle, and has often made as many enemies as he has friends because of his frankness on an issue. Porter has successfully fought off attacks by the press that he was an ineffective legislator. Yet "the Senator," as he is affectionately called by his friends, has enormous strengths. He knows his constituents and he knows Oklahoma politics. He can also argue issues effectively. Very importantly, Porter symbolizes power, especially when it involves the protection of minority rights. He acknowledges his controversial nature, but contends that that is the fate of those who lead. Whatever assessment one makes of Senator Porter, he and other black legislators have worked to advance the interest of the black community and the general good of the entire state.

Black Oklahomans have won election or appointment to state and local offices in increasing numbers since the mid-sixties. Historically, two of the most important appointments came with the selection of two jurists, Amos T. Hall and Charles L. Owens. Hall, of course, had won distinction in the *Sipuel* case. A native of Tulsa, he served as an attorney for the State Conference of Branches for the NAACP, and was a member of that national organization's legal committee. For eleven years he led the Tulsa NAACP. He spear-headed a number of civic functions including the capital-fund drive to build Carver Youth Center. For thirty-one years Hall was Grand Master of the Prince Hall Grand Lodge of the Oklahoma Masons; and he was a powerful figure in the Masons' national body. Following his appointment as Special Judge of the District Court of Tulsa County in 1969, he won election to office in his own right. In 1971, death interrupted his tenure on the bench. One writer summed up Hall's career very well when he said: "Few men in the history of Oklahoma have left their footprints on the sands of time in such varied and productive form as did Amos T. Hall."*

Charles Owens has also left his imprint on Oklahoma history. In 1968 Governor Dewey Bartlett selected Owens to fill the unexpired term of Judge Boston Smith of the Seventh Judicial District which covered Oklahoma and Canadian counties. As a result he became the first and only black to sit on a district court. Before the Tulsa native's appointment, he had served on the staff of the Oklahoma attorney general and had risen to chief of the criminal division. District judges, as with some others in Oklahoma, must stand for re-election although their jobs are not "political" in the sense that that term is often applied. In 1970 the people in Owen's predominantly white district gave him a more than two-to-one margin, and he duplicated this feat four years later. In 1978 he had no opposition for his seat on the bench, adequate testimony to his competency. From the beginning Owens expressed a desire to become a good judge, not simply a "good Negro judge." Only two other black judges have joined Owens and Hall in occupying a seat on a court in Oklahoma, Albert Alexander of Oklahoma City and Cecil Robinson of Muskogee. In the spring of 1979 the black community had high hopes that President Jimmy Carter would appoint a black, John Green, to the federal bench, but that likelihood faded when his name failed to be included among a list of possible appointees.

*From "Summary [of the activities] of Amos T. Hall" in Jimmy Stewart Collection, Black Heritage Chronicles, Ralph Ellison Branch, Oklahoma County Library System, Oklahoma City, Oklahoma.

Politically the black community has remained wedded to the Democratic party. Black Oklahomans, like blacks elsewhere, had shifted their allegiance from the Republican party in the 1930s. When editors Roscoe Dungee of the *Black Dispatch* and W. H. Twine of the Muskogee *Cimeter* dumped the GOP in 1932, their action served as a clear signal to other blacks in the state. By the election of 1936 the change had become obvious—the Republican party was dead within the black community. Blacks had turned Lincoln's picture to the wall. And they became an important part of the political coalition pieced together by Franklin D. Roosevelt and his New Dealers. The shift in parties had dramatic effects in the nation and in Oklahoma. Indeed, a Republican in Oklahoma became a rarity. Many blacks still argue that the Republican party is too conservative and is not in tune with the needs of the community. In recent years both the state and the national party have made attempts to attract black voters. Any dissatisfaction with Democrats among blacks, however, has usually been reflected by their refusal to vote rather than by turning to the Republicans or to a third party. The Republicans created a committee in the early seventies headed by Lennie Tolliver, a professor at the University of Oklahoma, to study ways to increase black participation in the party, but according to black leaders fundamental changes will have to take place before blacks shift their allegiance.

Advancements for blacks came not only in the political arena after the 1950s, but also in the economic sphere. The NAACP and other organizations fought for job opportunities to insure black folk a good, decent livelihood. They knew that to secure rights without the economic means of enjoying them would represent a hollow victory. Actually the demand for equal opportunity in jobs had been present for many years before the civil rights period of the sixties, but it intensified during that decade. In the mid-sixties the NAACP applied pressure upon large private businesses to hire and upgrade black people. The Urban League, as it had since its founding in the state in 1946, continued to work with the business community for the economic betterment of the black community. In the 1950s the League in Oklahoma City, its birthplace, successfully convinced the city to hire black bus drivers and firemen, and it persuaded a few labor unions to include bricklayers and carpenters in their ranks.

Despite advances it has been impossible to erase rapidly those economic problems which persist from past discrimination. Yet, improvements in income and in the quality of life among blacks are readily apparent. Federal and state programs have eliminated much poverty and have given blacks an economic boost, but the progress obtained has not been as encouraging as black leaders had hoped. They were particularly disappointed by the trend in the seventies which saw many of the gains of the sixties eroded. Inflation and a growing conservative mood among whites threatened to stifle the advances earlier realized during the civil rights crusade. Affirmative action programs, designed to give qualified women and minorities a special boost in job opportunities, came under attack. Many whites, including those who had profited from past discrimination, argued that such a program was wrong, that special privilege should go to no one. Black leaders contended that even though the chains of inequality had been removed from their people's legs, they could not catch up in the race for economic betterment until they had received assistance in arriving at the starting gate. It was unfair, they said in rebuttal to white opponents, to leave them mired in the problems which past injustice had created. By the 1970s black citizens were earning more income but they were still receiving less compared to whites. That was also true for both black and white families, but there was a greater difference in the disparity of income. And, not surprisingly, a much larger number of blacks appeared on the poverty rolls.

Black business in particular encountered staggering problems in the period after 1950. There was competition from white establishments, the lack of adequate resources and management skills, and the fear of embarking upon new or expanded operations. Tulsa's Greenwood district offered a striking commentary on the condition of black business. The area had contained some of the most prosperous businesses in the state before mid-century, but by the sixties Greenwood's decline had become noticeable to those who knew it well. By the latter part of the decade, for example, there were only six grocery stores where thirty-eight had stood twenty-five years earlier. Other examples highlighted the fact that as a business district the area was dying, one that had witnessed prosperity and had provided leisure and entertainment to thousands who lived in Oklahoma's "Oil City" and other parts of the state. Oklahoma City's famous Second Street had also dwindled in economic importance. In Muskogee, which prided itself as the hub of black business before statehood, there was little activity. State and federal programs and universities have directed attention toward the revitalization of black business, and the creation of new and more vigorous ones. But monumental problems exist. Perhaps the success of such enterprises as the Tulsa *Eagle,* the *Black Dispatch,* American Beauty Products, and Smokorama barbecue cooker will inspire aggressive, ambitious black businessmen. And the success of a minority financial institution such as Medical State Bank in Oklahoma City or American State Bank in Tulsa, could provide a "take-off" for those who formerly doubted their ability to compete in the world of "high finance." Certainly, the revival of black business could help give work to a community where the unemployment rate has traditionally been twice that of whites.

The desegregation of Oklahoma's schools in the 1960s and 1970s attracted much more public attention than the effort to revitalize business. The state moved forward without great difficulty in the years after 1955, but progress slowed significantly in the early sixties, and some resegregation appeared. The western portion contained few black children and the changes there did not create a great stir among whites. Most towns in eastern Oklahoma were relatively small, thus eliminating a number of thorny problems which faced Oklahoma's two largest school districts—Oklahoma City and Tulsa. When a federal district court ruled in the *Dowell* case in 1961 that Oklahoma City had to take measures to end segregation, it seemed that immediate integration of students and faculty would result. But that was not true, and the effort to achieve full integration continued to pose a challenge. In an effort to speed integration the city introduced the so-called "Finger Plan" which required busing.

Since 1972, both Oklahoma City and Tulsa have made advances in desegregating their schools. Proposals to rezone school districts in some cities of the state, however, have worried black leaders, for they see the possibility of resegregation.

At the college and university level the majority of black students attended integrated institutions by the end of the seventies. Langston remained predominantly black, as it always had been. It continued to be the center of much controversy. Changes in leadership, the building of new junior colleges which competed for the same students as Langston, a limited curriculum, the school's location, and diminishing support in certain quarters, all conspired to frustrate effective desegregation. Some politicians spoke of abolishing the institution or moving the black school to a metropolitan area. The creation of a branch at Tulsa, some say, was nothing more than a prelude to Langston's removal from its present location. Time will ultimately determine the university's fate. The battle over its welfare and its

74

right to survive does not only involve the issue of education, but the meaning of black heritage in Oklahoma, for Langston's graduates created many of the positive images which helped mold the black community.

BIBLIOGRAPHICAL ESSAY

Five general studies of varying quality are available for the reader interested in a fuller description of black life in Oklahoma. They are: Nathaniel J. Washington, *Historical Development of the Negro in Oklahoma* (Tulsa: Dexter Publishing Co., 1948); Gene Aldrich, *Black Heritage of Oklahoma* (Edmond: Thompson Book and Supply Co., 1973); Kaye M. Teall, ed., *Black History in Oklahoma—A Resource Book* (Oklahoma City: Oklahoma City Public Schools, 1971); Arthur L. Tolson, *The Black Oklahomans, A History: 1541–1972* (New Orleans: Edwards Printing Co., 1972); and Jimmie Lewis Franklin, *Journey Toward Hope: A History of Blacks in Oklahoma* (Norman: University of Oklahoma Press, in press). The bibliography and notes in the Franklin study provide the most comprehensive survey of the literature on black Oklahomans.

There is a small but growing number of specialized works on black people in the Sooner State. Rudi Halliburton has examined slavery in one of the Five Civilized Tribes in his *Red Over Black: Black Slavery Among the Cherokee Indians* (Westport, Conn.: Greenwood, 1977). The Halliburton study may be supplemented with two books by Daniel Littlefield, Jr., *The Cherokee Freedmen: From Emancipation to American Citizenship* (Westport: Greenwood, 1978); and his *Africans and Seminoles: From Emancipation to American Citizenship* (Westport: Greenwood, 1977). George Rawick, ed., *The American Slave: A Composite Autobiography. VII, Oklahoma and Mississippi Narratives* (Westport, Conn.: Greenwood, 1972), offers an inside view of slavery by those who lived through it. William Bittle and Gilbert Geis have written an excellent study of the Oklahoma Back-to-Africa movement in their *The Longest Way Home: Chief Alfred Sam's Back-to-Africa Movement* (Detroit: Wayne State University Press, 1964). This study is much broader than the title suggests, and it should hold the attention of those interested in black politics, economics, and social life in early-day Oklahoma. Professor Norman Crockett has looked at three of Oklahoma's black towns in *The Black Towns* (Lawrence: Regents Press of Kansas, 1979). Colonel Bailey C. Hanes has told a fascinating story of Oklahoma's famous black cowboy in his *Bill Pickett: Bulldogger* (Norman: University of Oklahoma Press, 1977). The life of Langston's noted poet is the concern of Neva J. Flasch in her *Melvin B. Tolson: A Critical Biography* (New York: Twayne, 1972). Ruth E. Swain captures the life and the struggle of the woman who integrated the University of Oklahoma Law School in *Ada Lois: The Sipuel Story* (New York: Vantage, 1978). George L. Cross, president of the University of Oklahoma at the time of Sipuel's entrance, shares his views of desegregation in his readable book, *Blacks in White Colleges: Oklahoma's Landmark Cases* (Norman: University of Oklahoma Press, 1975). Langston's history is told in Zella J. Black Patterson (with Lynnette L. Wert), *Langston University: A History* (Norman: University of Oklahoma Press, 1979). Integration in Oklahoma produced very little racial conflict but violence marked the state's early history. The story of the worst clash has been chronicled in Rudi Halliburton, *The Tulsa Race War of 1921* (San Francisco. R & E Associates, 1975). The dramatic history of the sit-in movement in Oklahoma and of civil rights after the fifties has drawn attention in Clara Luper, *Behold the Walls* (Oklahoma City: J. Wire, 1979).

Several books contain full chapters, or significant portions of chapters, devoted to segments of black life in Oklahoma. For example, William L. Katz, *The Black West* (Garden City: Doubleday, 1971), sketches some developments in prestatehood Oklahoma. Ralph Ellison discusses his early life and the people he knew in Oklahoma in *Shadow and Act* (New York: Random House, 1964). A thorough study of the Socialist party in Oklahoma is Garin Burbank's *When Farmers Voted Red: The Gospel of Socialism in the Oklahoma Countryside, 1910–1924* (Westport: Greenwood, 1977). Ross Russell, *Jazz Style in Kansas City and the Southwest* (Berkeley: University of California Press, 1971), has the best commentary on the Blue Devils and the musical era in which they lived. William Leckie has written a fine study of the black troops who helped police the frontier in his *The Buffalo Soldiers: A Narrative of the Negro Cavalry in the West* (Norman: University of Oklahoma Press, 1967).

A small number of journals have articles on black Oklahoma. The Franklin study cited above is a good reference for the beginning student or the general reader. The most useful journals are: *Harlow's*

Weekly, Journal of Negro History, Journal of Negro Education, Crisis (NAACP), *Opportunity* (Urban League), *Progress Magazine, Black Voices,* and the *Chronicles of Oklahoma.* Even a brief examination of available theses, old newspapers, documents, and other original sources can whet the appetite for more serious investigation of particular topics. The best guide to theses are Vicki Withers, "A Checklist of Theses and Dissertations Relating to Oklahoma History Completed at the University of Oklahoma and Oklahoma State University Through 1973" (Master's thesis, Oklahoma State University, 1974), and Patrick Blessing, *Oklahoma: Records and Archives* (Tulsa: University of Tulsa Publications in American Social History, 1978). Oklahoma probably had as many black newspapers before 1930 as any other state. Although many of them are now lost, the Oklahoma Historical Society has a microfilm collection which includes about thirty of those papers. The most complete holdings are the Oklahoma City *Black Dispatch* and the Tulsa *Eagle.* Finally, two valuable collections of manuscripts are easily available to the reader or researcher who desires them. They are the Works Progress Administration Records at the Oklahoma Historical Society in Oklahoma City, and the Jimmy Stewart Papers of the Black Heritage Chronicles of Oklahoma at the Ralph Ellison Branch of the Oklahoma City Public Library. Other files and manuscript holdings at universities, the Oklahoma Historical Society, and the Oklahoma State Library will yield scattered pieces of materials on black Oklahoma. Langston University has given special attention to the collection of historical items on black culture in the state, but progress has been slow. The increasing availability of documents, and an appreciation for keeping them in good condition, will enable future historians to recreate the past. Young students and others interested in the study of history could make a significant contribution to scholarship by initiating a program for the collection and the maintenance of materials on black people in their community; or they could support projects already in operation. Such efforts would help scholars round out the black image in Oklahoma.

LaVergne, TN USA
22 January 2011
213562LV00002B/1/P